VEGAN

30 Days of Vegan Recipes and Meal Plans for Increasing Your Health and Energy

© **Copyright 2017 by Mastermind Self Development- All rights reserved.**

The follow eBook is reproduced below with the goal of providing information that is as accurate and reliable as possible. Regardless, purchasing this eBook can be seen as consent to the fact that both the publisher and the author of this book are in no way experts on the topics discussed within and that any recommendations or suggestions that are made herein are for entertainment purposes only. Professionals should be consulted as needed prior to undertaking any of the action endorsed herein.

This declaration is deemed fair and valid by both the American Bar Association and the Committee of Publishers Association and is legally binding throughout the United States.

Furthermore, the transmission, duplication or reproduction of any of the following work including specific information will be considered an illegal act irrespective of if it is done electronically or in print. This extends to creating a secondary or tertiary copy of the work or a recorded copy and is only allowed with express written consent from the Publisher. All additional right reserved.

The information in the following pages is broadly considered to be a truthful and accurate account of facts and as such any inattention, use or misuse of the information in question by the reader will render any resulting actions solely under their purview. There are no scenarios in which the publisher or the original author of this work can be in any fashion deemed liable for any hardship or damages that may befall them after undertaking information described herein.

Additionally, the information in the following pages is intended only for informational purposes and should thus be thought of as universal. As befitting its nature, it is presented without assurance regarding its prolonged validity or interim quality. Trademarks that are mentioned are done without written consent and can in no way be considered an endorsement from the trademark holder.

Free membership into the Mastermind Self Development Group!

For a limited time, you can join the Mastermind Self Development Group for free! You will receive videos and articles from top authorities in self development as well as a special group only offers on new books and training programs. There will also be a monthly member only draw that gives you a chance to win any book from your Kindle wish list!

If you sign up through this link http://www.mastermindselfdevelopment.com/specialreport you will also get a special free report on the Wheel of Life. This report will give you a visual look at your current life and then take you through a series of exercises that will help you plan what your perfect life looks like. The workbook does not end there; we then take you through a process to help you plan how to achieve that perfect life. The process is very powerful and has the potential to change your life forever. Join the group now and start to change your life!
http://www.mastermindselfdevelopment.com/specialreport

Introduction

Chapter 1: Why to Go Vegan

Chapter 2: Understanding Vegan Diets

Chapter 3: Meal Plan and Outline Recipes for Block I
- Day 1
- Day 2
- Day 3
- Day 4
- Day 5
- Day 6
- Day 7
- Day 8

Chapter 4: Meal Plan and Outline Recipes for Block II
- Day 9
- Day 10
- Day 11
- Day 12
- Day 13
- Day 14
- Day 15
- Day 16

Chapter 5: Meal Plan and Recipes for Block III
- Day 17
- Day 18
- Day 19
- Day 20
- Day 21
- Day 22
- Day 23

Chapter 6: Meal Plan and Recipes for Block IV
- Day 24
- Day 25
- Day 26
- Day 27
- Day 28
- Day 29
- Day 30

Conclusion – How to Stay Committed

Introduction

Veganism is fast catching up with many people across the world. The noble idea behind veganism such as not wanting to exploit the less fortunate animal species of the world by taking what is theirs and selfishly using it for ourselves simply because they do not have the power to stop us is, perhaps, the primary reason for the growth in popularity of this concept.

However, in addition to the above extremely thoughtful reason, the health benefits and other great things about veganism are all sufficiently powerful causes for the expansion of the idea of veganism across the planet. This book is written with an intention to exhort newcomers to try a one-month vegan challenge that has the power to change not just your lifestyle but your entire outlook on life.

Before you decide to try to change your lifestyle to vegan, there are a few things you must know and understand about it. This book aims to do exactly that by giving you a detailed overview in the following areas:

- What is veganism?
- A brief history on veganism
- How is veganism useful to you?
- Meal Plans for a one-month challenge along with recipe outlines
- How to stay committed to the cause?

What is veganism?

You know who are vegetarians? They do not consume poultry, meat, or, fish in their diet. Vegans, additionally, do not consume or use any animal products and/or by-products such as dairy products, honey, eggs, leather, silk, fur, and soaps and cosmetics made from animal sources. Vegans are the superset of vegetarians. All vegans are also vegetarians but all vegetarians need not be vegans.

Vegans believe that veganism is not just about their diet but a way of life. As far as possible, vegans avoid exploitation of animals in any form including but not limited to food, clothing, or other purposes. They also avoid items that have been tested on animals before being commercialized. And believe it or not, there is a vegan diet for all kinds of diets ranging from the junk food lovers to the raw food lovers and those in between, too.

History of Veganism

Veganism, although not known as veganism, has been around for many centuries. Examples of prevention of exploitation against and cruelty to animals have been written in history books. Lord Buddha of India and Pythagoras both advocated this concept and had put in rules to ensure their followers ate only plant-based food and completely avoided meats and animal products.

The earliest modern-day veganism is known to have occurred around 1806 CE. During that time, the great English poet P B Shelley and Dr. William Lambe publicly objected to consuming dairy products and eggs by humans on ethical grounds. This incident seems to have laid the foundation for modern-day veganism.

In November 1944, six non-dairy vegetarians including Donald Watson and Elsie Shrigley called met together and discussed the topic on non-dairy vegetarians' lifestyles and diets. Despite strong opposition, these six members founded the new movement and became actively involved in this new project.

When the Vegan Society was formalized and registered as a charity organization in 1979, the Memorandum and Articles of Association of the society defined veganism as:

"...a philosophy and way of living which seeks to exclude – as far as possible and practicable – all forms of exploitation of, and cruelty to, animals for food, clothing or any other purpose; and by extension, promotes the development and use of animal-free alternatives for the benefit of humans, animals, and the environment. In dietary terms, it denotes the practice of dispensing with all products derived wholly or partly from animals."

This book deals only with the dietary aspect of veganism giving you amply sufficient reasons to shift your lifestyle to this healthy and noble one. While the benefits of turning vegan are discussed in another chapter, the kind of foods that you can include in your diet while keeping your energy levels and health not just unchanged but also improved than earlier is huge.

Here is a small list of foods that are known to be totally vegan:

- All kinds of grains and cereals
- All kinds of beans and legumes
- All fruits and vegetables

Other vegan foods include soy milk, vegan mayonnaise, vegan ice cream and cheese, vegan hot dogs, and more. Moreover, a lot of companies have come out with mock meats that give vegans a sense of eating meat. This book also has 4 chapters dedicated to making vegan foods, which includes easy-to-make recipes.

Chapter 1: Why Go Vegan?

Most people in the world want to do the following things by some means or the other:

- Lose weight
- Eat better
- Get fitter and healthier
- Do something for society and the world at large

The great news is that if you shift to a vegan diet, you can achieve all the above goals. And let me assure you, you will enjoy delicious, wholesome, and satiating meals as well.

No loss or reduction in energy levels – There is a misconception that changing to vegan diet reduces your energy levels. There are numerous unworthy talks of vegans living only on water and a few greens and hence their energy levels have taken a huge dip. And on the other side of the spectrum, there are plenty of spurious rumors that talk of people going vegan is helping them do impossible things. These other-end-of-the-spectrum talks make out vegans to be people who can walk on water! Let me assure you that neither of the extremes is true or based on any scientific studies.

Health benefits are huge when you choose to go vegan. Of course, the initial learning curve is going to be steep and you would have to counter multiple challenges. However, once you have overcome these tough phases and complete the 30-day challenge, you are going feel to fitter, lighter, and happier. Moreover, there are multiple studies done by various organizations including the British Dietetic Association that has proven the excellent efficacies of getting fitter and healthier by following a vegan diet.

Here is the list of a few magic foods that can restore energy instantaneously:

Bananas – Already beautifully and naturally packaged by nature, this wonderful tropical fruit is normally the first you must reach out for when you feel tired or fatigued.

Walnuts – Another great pick-me-up tree nut, walnuts are rich in plant proteins, omega fatty acids, and vitamins giving you the almost-instant energy boost.

Green smoothies – Delicious smoothies made by tossing together strawberries, bananas, and orange juices are great and extremely healthy pick-me-ups to fight fatigue.

Coconut water – This is nature's energy drink and is amazingly refreshing and is filled with vitamins and potassium.

Kiwi – This low-fat delicious fruit is an instant energy enhancer triggered by the simple sugars present in it.

Why I chose to mention vegan energy boosters in the beginning itself is to help you overcome doubts regarding your ability to get on with your daily schedule if you choose to go vegan. Today there are many sportspeople who have shifted to this diet to keep fitter and sustain energy levels. So, if highly active people in the field of sports can take advantage of veganism, it should not be difficult for moderately active people like us to take this 30-day challenge and come out with flying colors.

Other great reasons to take the one-month challenge to go vegan are:

Lose weight and yet remain energized – Many of us love to find a sensible way to lose excess weight and yet remain healthy and fit. Average vegans are known to weigh 20 pounds lesser than average meat-eaters. Despite this, vegan diets do not starve you and make you feel enervated like the usual run-of-the-meal fad diets do.

Keep diseases and health disorders away – The Academy of Nutrition and Dietetics have conducted multiple studies which show that taking the vegan route helps you steer clear of common disorders such as diabetes, hypertension or high blood pressure thereby preventing the onset of many modern-day diseases such as heart attacks, kidney failure, and others.

Vegan foods are yummy and delicious – If you thought going vegan means you would have to give up your favorite ice creams, hamburgers, and chicken sandwiches, then you are wrong. With demand for vegan products soaring, many companies are coming up with amazingly delicious vegan options that taste very much like the non-vegetarian stuff. You will not miss any of the meats and animal products at all. There are plenty of established brands that cater to veganism and deliver really tasty dairy and meat substitutes.

Vegan diets are full of highly nutritious and healthy food items including whole grains, beans and legumes, nuts, soy products, and fresh fruits and vegetables. Here are some of the health benefits that these fiber-rich and healthy food sources provide you with:

- **Minimal saturated fats** – Meats and dairy products contain plenty of saturated fats thereby increasing the risk of cardiovascular diseases. Vegan diets automatically reduce intake of saturated fats enhancing your health condition

- **Fiber** – A vegan diet is high in fiber content that is very conducive to healthy bowel movements.

- **Magnesium** – Dark, green leafy vegetables are a rich source of magnesium, a key element that aids the body in the absorption of calcium.

- **Potassium** – Similarly, potassium, an important mineral that balances acidity and water in our body and helps in the removal of toxins is found in plenty in plant-based foods.

- **Proteins** – Meat-eaters invariably end up with more proteins than is needed by the body. Vegan diets, which include nuts, beans, and legumes, have the right amount of proteins for us.

Vegan diets provide other critically essential nutrients such as Vitamins E and C, phytochemicals, antioxidants, and foliates. These help in keeping your immunity system healthy and robust and also prevent age-related diseases such as Alzheimer's and Parkinson's disease and keep your overall body organs functioning well.

Vegan diets have the power to prevent the following diseases that are very common in today's high-stressed unhealthy lifestyle:

- Cardiovascular diseases
- Reduced cholesterol due to the complete absence of meat and dairy products in your diet
- Age-related macular degeneration
- Reduced risk of breast cancer
- Reduced risk of contracting ailments like diabetes, hypertension, cataracts, colon and prostate cancer, arthritis, and osteoporosis

In addition to improved health and prevention of diseases, going vegan makes you stronger, more energetic, and more attractive. Here is how:

Lowered Body Mass Index – A diet without meat and dairy products automatically help in the reduction of body mass index

Weight loss – Weight loss is an unquestioned effect of a vegan diet.

Healthy skin – Consuming rich sources of Vitamins A and E from nuts and fruits and vegetables enhance the texture and health of your skin.

Reduced allergy symptoms – Plant-based foods do not trigger as many allergic reactions in humans as dairy and meat products do.

Less intake of mercury – A lot of shellfish and fish contain high levels of mercury, which we take in when we eat these foods. Switching to veganism does away with this toxin completely.

The above are only some of the great reasons that you must start off this 30-day vegan challenge. Instead of finding reasons not to do something good, focus on the above reasons which tell you why you should do it and dive straight in. Summon some extra willpower from yourself and after you complete this challenge you can rest assured that the willpower would come on its own when you see and feel the wondrous new VEGAN YOU.

Chapter 2: Understanding Vegan Diets

In the previous chapter, along with why should you go vegan, I had mentioned some basic foods that can deliver instant energy whenever you feel enervated. Just to reiterate, the foods listed are all completely vegan and yet are employed by all to get back energy levels when they feel sapped.

Considering the huge amount of misconception, doubts, and skepticism regarding energy levels and maintenance of good health by vegan, I thought it made sense to dedicate one chapter to help you overcome these misunderstandings which in turn will, I hope, will catapult your move to try out the 30-day vegan challenge.

There are many ex-vegans who complain of fogginess, depression, and other challenging mental and social circumstances when they chose to give up animal foods. Understanding the power and function of each nutrient is highly helpful in managing those seemingly difficult days especially during the initial days when support system and a common social network help you understand the root cause the issues and get you an objective and tried-and-tested solution.

Knowing how the various nutrients derived from animal and plant sources differ from each other, which vegan foods give you optimum results and how to keep feelings of depression due to short-term failures at bay are all critical elements in making a success of your 30-day vegan challenge. And when you come out successful in a small attempt, you will be emboldened to try for something bigger.

Carbohydrates for vegans – Cutting back on carbohydrates for anyone is not that difficult for anyone including for us vegans. It is essential for you to use low-carb food sources to maintain good health with a vegan diet.

Vegetables: There are many vegetables which are low-carb foods including onions, tomatoes, eggplant, cauliflower, broccoli, bell peppers, and more.

Fruits: Blueberries and strawberries are low-carb foods. However, depending on how much you need daily, other fruits can easily be included.

Fatty foods – Olives and avocados are high in good fats and low-carb too and hence excellent dietary inclusions for vegans.

Soy, nuts, and seeds: These are low in carbohydrates and high in fats and proteins. So, it is imperative to include soy, soy-based foods, nuts, and seeds into your daily diet.

Chia seeds: I deliberately included this one special item because most of the carbohydrates in chia seeds are in the form of fiber. Hence, most of the energy source from this food is got from fats and proteins. Do include chia seeds whenever you can.

Additionally, choose slow carbohydrate foods, that is, consume carb sources that have a low glycemic index. These foods prevent high fluctuations in your blood sugar levels and you will feel more satiated over a longer period as they release glucose slowly. For instance, choose breads that have been made from non-ground grains, use barley, quinoa, and oats in place of rice, use fresh beans and legumes instead of canned ones, use sweet potatoes instead of white potatoes.

Animal Protein Vs. Plant Protein – As our body does not accumulate protein, it is imperative that we take in proteins in our daily diet. Proteins are available both in plant-based and animal-based foods. The different between the two sources is the profile of amino acid present. Amino acids are of different types (about 20 of them are very critical for us) and all of them are essential for carrying out multiple metabolic activities in our body.

Animal proteins invariably have a sufficiently wide of range of amino acids in them whereas many plant proteins are not complete. For instance, many plant proteins are quite low in important amino acids such as tryptophan, methionine, isoleucine, and lysine, Legumes, on the other hand, are the best plant-based protein source that is comparable to meats. For this express reason, ensure you eat 3 servings of legumes daily in the form of peas, beans, peanuts, tofu etc. This will keep you energy levels optimum and considerably reduce your craving for meats.

Fats in vegan diets – Very low-fat foods are not great for vegan diets. In fact, a lot of recent studies have proved that very low-fat diets are not effective in the long-term. However, a free-for-all fatty diet is also an absolute no-no. It is important to include good-fat foods such as nuts and avocados to get the right quality and quantity of fat. Nutrition experts believe you should consume not more than 30 gm. of saturated fats every day.

Vitamins, Omega-3 fats, and other important nutrients – Animal protein foods contain higher levels and a wider range of other important nutrients such as Vitamins (B12 and D), DHA (Docosahexaenoic acid), which is an essential omega-3 fatty acid, zinc, and heme-iron. The four listed nutrients are found in abundance in meats such as pork, beef, dairy products, eggs, and fish, but are a little low in plant-based foods.

While this may seem a concern, let me assure you that there are ample solutions for this other than simply giving up a fantastically healthy lifestyle that has the power to change multiple things in a positive way (already discussed in the previous chapter). Omega-3 fatty acids are available in plenty in walnuts, flaxseed and flaxseed oil, and chia seeds. Vitamin B12 plant-based analogs include sourdough bread, fermented soy foods, shiitake mushrooms, and sea vegetables. Moreover, these trace nutritional elements like Vitamin B12, Vitamin D, iodine etc. can be easily taken as supplements.

Most plant-based foods are rich in folate (dark, green leafy veggies provide this nutrient in plenty), potassium, calcium (figs, nuts, almonds etc. are wonderfully rich in calcium), iron (lentils are a great source) Vitamin C, phytochemicals, and Vitamin A (carrots). So these nutrients are well covered in a vegan diet through the intake of ample amounts of differently colored fruits and vegetables.

Do not hesitate to use convenience foods – There are plenty of convenience products for vegans available in the market today. These include vegan ice creams, vegan meats, and vegan cheeses. When you are pressed for time and need convenience over laborious cooking processes, do not hesitate to use these options as they will go a long way in helping you stay committed to the vegan cause especially in the early days when you are suntil in the learning curve.

Chapter 3: Meal Plan and Outline Recipes for Block I

The next few chapters are dedicated to giving you meal plans along with some basic recipes and motivation for the start of your 30-day vegan challenge journey.

Day 1

"The secret of getting ahead is getting started."

- *Mark Twain*

Green smoothies for Breakfast

What to use:
- Mango juice (1/4 cup)
- Coconut Water (1/2 cup)
- Parsley (1/2 cup, fresh)
- Cilantro (1/2 cup, fresh)
- Avocado (1/2 – 1)
- Ice

What to do:
In a blender, mix mango juice and coconut water until the two are smoothly blended. Now add parsley, cilantro, avocado, and ice cubes and blend again to get a thick, super smooth smoothie. Adjust tartness and sweetness levels with sweetener choice to match your liking.

Lemon and Citrus Couscous with Fennel and Chickpeas for Lunch

What to use:
- Fennel (1 cup, trimmed)
- Chickpeas (2 cups, cooked)
- Coriander (1/4 cup)
- Couscous (3 cups)
- Lemon Juice (1 tbsp.)
- Kalamata Olives (1/3 cup)
- Orange Juice (1/3 cup)
- Citrus zest (1 ½ tbsp.)
- Olive oil (3 tbsp.)

What to do:

In a pan, cook the trimmed fennel until it reaches caramelization. To this, add cooked chickpeas, ground coriander, lemon juice, and kalamata olives and continue cooking over a medium flame until you have a nice veggie-filled sauce. To give the couscous a citrusy flavor, cook it in a mixture of orange juice and water along with some lemon and orange zest, a little olive oil, and salt. To serve this couscous meal, fluff up the couscous using a fork. Make a layer of the couscous plate and over it, spoon out the fennel and chickpeas mixture. You can now use the fennel frond for garnishing. Dig into your delicious vegan lunch.

Tofu-Spinach Lasagna for Dinner -

What to Use:
- Lasagna noodles (24 oz.)
- Spinach (12 oz., frozen, chopped)
- Tofu (12 oz.)
- Sugar (1/4 tsp.)
- Soymilk (
- Lemon Juice (1 tbsp.)
- Garlic powder (1 tbsp.)
- Salt (1/2 tsp.)
- Basil (1 cup)
- Tomato Sauce (1 ½ cups)

What to do:
Cook the lasagna noodles as directed on the package, drain and keep aside. Squeeze the spinach to remove water as much as possible. In a blender, blitz together sugar, tofu, soymilk, lemon juice, garlic powder, salt, and basil until you get a smooth blend. Now, stir in the dried spinach. Take a baking dish and make a layer of tomato sauce at the bottom. Make a layer of the cooked lasagna noodles over this and over this a layer of the tofu mixture. Repeat the three layers again until all the materials are used up. The top layer should be that of the noodles and tomato sauce poured over it. In a preheated oven, bake this for about 25-30 minutes. Enjoy.

Day 2

"A wise man should consider that health is the greatest of human blessings, and learn how by his own thought to derive benefit from his illnesses."

- *Hippocrates*

Mango Smoothie for Breakfast -

What to use:
- Mango (frozen, 2 cups)
- Orange juice (1 ½ cups)
- Lime zest (½ tsp)
- Maple syrup (pure)

What to do:
Add 2 cups frozen mango, 1 ½ cup orange juice, ½ cup avocado, ½ tsp lime zest, pure maple syrup (to taste), and appropriate amount of water into a blender and blitz together everything until you get a lovely, thick, and creamy smoothie

Avocado and sauerkraut sandwiches for lunch -

What to Use:
- Dijon mustard (to taste)
- Bread (pumpernickel or rye)
- Vegan Thousand Island dressing (to taste)
- Sauerkraut (2 oz.)
- Avocado (1/2)

What to do:
Spread Dijon mustard on one slice of pumpernickel or rye bread and spread Thousand Island vegan dressing on the other slice. On an oiled (lightly) skillet, place the two slices (dry side down) and grill until golden brown. Pile on sauerkraut topping for one slice and avocado on the other slice. Continue to grill over medium heat for about 5 minutes. Remove from heat and join two halves and enjoy. Combine with cucumber and tomato salad for a complete vegan meal.

Scallion Pancakes for Dinner -

What to use:
- All-purpose flour (2 cups)
- Vegetable shortening (2 tbsp.)
- Salt (1/2 tsp.)
- Green Onions (1 ½ cups)
- Oil (1/4 cup)

What to do:
Make pancake dough with all-purpose flour, knead well and keep aside for some time. Then roll out the dough (1/8-inch thickness); spread a layer of vegetable shortening, and then sprinkle a layer of salt and then a layer of green onions. Gently roll this into a jelly-shaped roll and cut out fist-sized pieces. Again, with rolling pin, roll out each piece into 1/8-inch thick slices and cook on an oiled skillet until both sides for about 2 minutes each. Place the cooked pancakes on paper tissues to remove the excess oil and dig in. You could use soy sauce as a tartar dip.

Day 3

"If you're happy, if you're feeling good, then nothing else matters."

- *Robin Wright*

Chocolate Hemp Smoothie for Breakfast –

What to use:
- Almond Milk (2 cups)
- Pitted Dates (1/3 cup)
- Unsweetened cocoa powder (3 tbsp)
- Hemp seeds (3 tbsp)
- Banana (1, whole)
- Cinnamon (¼ tbsp)
- Ice

What to do:
In a blender add almond milk (2 cups), 1/3 cup pitted dates, 3 tbsp. unsweetened cocoa powder, 3 tbsp. hemp seeds (hulled), 1 banana (peeled and cut into slices/cubes), ¼ tsp cinnamon powder, and ice cubes. Blend it all together until the mixture reaches a thick, creamy, and smoothie-like (though this will be of a slightly thinner consistency) consistency. Pour into a glass and drink away.

Minestrone Soup and Crusty Bread for Lunch –

What to use:
- Olive oil (1 tbsp.)
- Onions (¾ cup, chopped)
- Zucchini (1/2 diced)
- Carrots (2, chopped)
- Beans (3 cups)
- Tomatoes (1 diced)
- Garlic (1 clove, minced)
- Celery (2 stalks, diced)
- Basil (1/4 cup)
- Pepper (1 tsp.)
- Salt (2/3 tsp.)
- Oregano (1 tsp.)

- Water (6 cups)
- Macaroni noodles (¼ cup)

What to do:
In a saucepan, heat 1 tbsp. of olive oil (extra virgin) over medium heat. Sauté ¾ cup finely chopped onions, and add the following water, diced zucchini, carrots, beans, diced tomatoes, minced garlic, diced celery, dried basil, and pepper, oregano, and salt. Bring all this to a boil, and simmer for about 25-30 minutes until all ingredients are cooked. Now add ¼ cup macaroni and cook for another 10 minutes. Adjust spices to your taste and serve hot with some pumpernickel or rye bread (roasted on a skillet with a dash of oil).

Vegan sausages for dinner -

What to use:
- Beans (2 cups, personal choice for base)
- Olive oil (2 tsp.)
- Soy sauce (2 tbsp.)
- Garlic (1 bulb, minced)
- Wheat gluten (1 tsp.)
- Yeast (1 tsp.)
- Fennel seeds (1/3 cup, crushed)
- Red pepper flakes (1/2 tbsp.)
- Pepper (2 tbsp.)
- Oregano (2 tbsp.)
- Salt (1 tbsp.)

What to do:
Get your steaming apparatus ready with water brought to a full boil. Cool and mash your chosen beans for a base nicely until no lumps are left. Add olive oil, soy sauce, finely minced garlic, wheat gluten, nutritional yeast, crushed fennel seeds, red pepper flakes, pepper, oregano, and salt and mix well until you get nice smooth dough-like consistency. Divide this dough into 4-6 portions and make each portion into a log shape (like the meat sausages). Place these on separate tin foils and roll the foil to look like a tootsie roll. Put these wrapped vegan sausages in the steamer and cook for about 40 minutes. Remove from heat and your vegan sausages are ready. Serve hot with a nice soy sauce dip or simply with ketchup.

Day 4

"Veganism is not a sacrifice. It is a joy."

- *Gary L. Francion*

Peanut Butter Banana Smoothie for Breakfast –

What to use:
- Bananas (2 whole, frozen)
- Dates (4 whole)
- Peanut butter (1 tbsp)
- Chia seeds (1 tbsp)
- Water (¼ cup)

What to do:
In a blender, add 2 sliced frozen bananas, 4 small dates, 1 tbsp. peanut butter, 1 tbsp. chia seeds, and ¼ cup water. Blitz together until well blended and your smoothie is ready.

Asparagus, Potato, and Squash Frittata for Lunch -

Ingredients:

Squash (1, sliced)
Potatoes (2 sliced)
Garlics (1 bulb, minced)
Italian Herbs (1 tsp.)
Onion (1/2 onion)
Salt (1 tsp.)
Pepper (2 tbsp.)
Asparagus (12 oz.)
Tofu (8 oz.)

Fry the squash and potatoes until golden brown. To this add garlic, dried herbs, and onions and continue to sauté until the onions are soft. Add salt and pepper for seasoning. Now, put in the asparagus and stir over heat for a couple more minutes. Put this veggie mixture into cake tin. In a blender, blitz together tofu and other remaining ingredients (except the dried herbs) until smooth. Now add the herbs and mix well. Pour this tofu mixture onto the veggie layer. Smoothen out the tofu layer with a knife and bake for 30-40 minutes in a medium heat oven.

Tempeh Casserole for Dinner -

What to use:
- Tempeh (8 oz.)
- Onions (1 diced)
- Zucchini (1 sliced)
- Broccoli stock (2 cups)
- Brown rice (2 cups)
- Arrowroot starch (1 tbsp.)
- Balsamic vinegar (3 tbsp.)
- Herbs (2 tbsp.)
- Baking powder (1 tbsp.)
- Egg Substitute (1/4 cup)
- Vegan mayo (3 tsp.)
- Paprika (1/2 tsp.)
- Salt (1/4 tsp.)

What to do:
Mash the tempeh either in a food processor or with a potato masher. In a big bowl, mix this mashed tempeh with onions, zucchini, broccoli stock, brown rice, arrowroot starch, balsamic vinegar, herbs, baking powder, and egg substitute and place in a casserole dish. In a preheated oven at 350F, cook for about 20 minutes. For the sauce, combine vegan mayo, paprika, and salt. Serve hot.

Day 5

"As I improved my diet, I started to learn to love my self, probably for the first time ever."

- *Frank Ferrante*

Strawberry and Avocado Smoothie for Breakfast –

What to use:
- Banana (1/2 frozen)
- Strawberries (fresh, 2 cups)
- Spearmint (3 tbsp)
- Coconut water (1 ½ cups)
- Avocado (1/2)
- Date (pitted)
- Ice

What to do:
In a food processor, blend together ½ a frozen banana, 2 cups of fresh strawberries, 3 tbsp. of spearmint, 1 ½ cups of coconut water, ½ an avocado, 1 pitted date, and ice cubes. Your smoothie is ready to drink.

Adzuki Bean Burgers with Potato Wedges for Lunch -

What to use:
- Oats (1 package, prepackaged)
- Olive oil (1 tsp.)
- Celery (2 stalks, finely chopped)
- Onion (chopped)
- Garlic (1 bulb)
- Carrots (2 chopped)
- Salt (1 tbsp.)
- Basil (3 tbsp.)
- Water (2 cups)
- Adzuki beans (1 cup)
- Parsley (2 tbsp.)
- Brown rice flour (1/4 cup)
- Bread (rye or pumpernickel)

What to do:
Boil the water in a saucepan and add a packet of oats. Simmer for about 2 minutes until the oats are cooked. Over a medium flame, heat 2 tbsp. of olive oil and put in celery, onions, garlic, and carrots and cook until tender. Add a little water, salt and basil to this mixture and stir occasionally and cook for another 5 minutes.

In a food processor, blitz together the onion mixture, cooked oats, adzuki beans, and parsley. Stir in the brown rice flour until you get a dough-like consistency that can be molded into patties. Form 8-10 patties with this. Cook the patties on a skillet with a dash of oil. Place between toasted pumpernickel or rye bread and enjoy your meal.

Lentil and Barley Casserole for Dinner -

What to use:
- Oil (2 tbsp.)
- Onions (1 diced)
- Garlic (2 bulbs, minced)
- Potatoes (3 diced)
- Swede (3 oz.)
- Carrots (3 chunked
- Rosemary (1 oz.)
- Bay leaves (1 oz.)
- Thyme (1 oz.)
- Tomato paste (1 cup)
- Water (2 cup)
- Pearl barley (2 oz.)
- Lentils (1/2 cup)
- Stock powder and cube (1 prepackaged)
- Mushrooms (2/3 cup)
- Pepper (1 tbsp.)

What to do:
In a large pan, heat oil and sauté the onions and garlic. Add potatoes, swede, and carrots (all cut into large chunks) and continue cooking until the veggies get tender. Put in rosemary, bay leaves, thyme, and tomato paste. Pour 5 cups of water and add pearl barley, lentils, stock powder, stock cube, and mushrooms. Add a little pepper for seasoning. Bring this mixture to a boil and then simmer over a low flame for about 45 minutes until a casserole consistency is achieved. Remove the bay leaves and then serve.

Day 6

"It's not a diet. It's not a phase. It's a permanent lifestyle."

- *Anonymous*

Cherry limeade Smoothie for Breakfast –

What to use:
- Peach (1 sliced)
- Cherries (frozen, 1 cup)
- Almond milk (¾ cup)
- Lime juice (1 lime, fresh squeezed)
- Ice

What to do:
In a blender, blend together 1 ripe peach (sliced), 1 cup frozen cherries, ¾ cup almond milk, juice of 1 lime, and some ice cubes. Your smoothie is ready.

Baked Potatoes and Coleslaw for Lunch -

What to use:
- Olive oil (1 tbsp.)
- Potatoes (6 whole)
- Vegan cream cheese (3 oz.)
- Vegan mayo (4 tsp.)
- Mustard (3 tsp.)
- Cabbage (2 cups, chopped)
- Carrots (1 cup, chopped)
- Onions (2/3 cup, chopped)

What to do:
Smear a little olive oil on the washed and dried potatoes and bake in a preheated oven for about 1 to 1 ½ hours until soft on the inside and crisp on the outside. For the coleslaw, combine cream cheese, vegan mayonnaise, and mustard until you get a smooth mixture. Add this to finely chopped cabbage, carrots, and onions, and mix well. Season as needed and refrigerate. When the potatoes are ready, cut in the middle and add the coleslaw and serve.

Noodles with vegetables and tofu for dinner -

What you need:
- Soy sauce (4 tsp.)
- Sweet chili sauce (2 tsp.)
- Mushroom sauce (2 tsp.)
- Noodles (24 oz.)
- olive oil (1 tsp.)
- Onions (1/2, chopped)
- Ginger (1 oz. grated)
- Garlic (1 bulb, minced)
- Vegetables of choice
- Tofu (12 oz.)

What to do:
In a small bowl, mix together soy sauce, sweet chili sauce, and vegetarian mushroom sauce. In a large bowl, put a packet of noodles and cover completely with hot water. Close with a lid and set aside. Heat olive oil in a saucepan or wok and stir fry chopped onions for a minute. Now add ginger, garlic and vegetables of your choice (such as carrots, zucchini, red capsicum, and broccoli for example). Add some tofu too and fry for a further 2-3 minutes. Use 5-spice powder for seasoning. Drain the liquid from the bowl of noodles. After removing all the water, add the noodles into the wok. Add the sauce mixture and mix everything well. Cook for another minute or two and serve hot.

Day 7

"When diet is wrong, medicine is of no use. When diet is correct, medicine is of no need."

- *Ayurvedic proverb*

Creamy Chocolate Shake for Breakfast –

What you need:
- Bananas (2, frozen)
- Strawberries (⅓ cup, frozen)
- Unsweetened cocoa powder (2-3 tbsp)
- Almond butter (2 tbsp)
- Flaxseed (1 tbsp)
- Non-dairy milk (1 ½-2 cups)
- Sweetener
- Ice

What to do:
In a blender, blitz together 2 ripe frozen bananas, 1/3 cup frozen strawberries, 2-3 tbsp. pure unsweetened cocoa powder, 2 tbsp. almond butter (salted), 1 tbsp. flaxseed meal, 1 ½ - 2 cups almond milk or soy milk or coconut milk, a dash of agave nectar or stevia, and some ice cubes. Your shake is ready

Vegetable and Pesto Sandwich for Lunch –

What you need:
- Zucchini (1 sliced)
- Eggplant (1 sliced)
- Capsicum (4 oz.)
- Onions (1 chopped)
- Pepper (2 tbsp.)
- Salt (1 tbsp.)
- Olive oil (1 tsp.)
- Pesto (dairy-free, to taste)
- Bread
- Lettuce (1 large leaf)
- Tomato (2 slices)

What to do:
Roast zucchini, eggplant, capsicum, and onions along with seasoning of pepper, salt and olive oil in an oven until they turn soft and lightly brown. Spread dairy-free pesto on two bread slices and pile on the roasted veggies, tomato slices, and some lettuce leaves. Bring the slices together and your yummy veggie sandwich is ready.

***Shepherd's pie for Dinner* –**

What you need:
- Potatoes (5)
- Salt (2 tsp.)
- Vegan margarine (3 oz.)
- Onions (1 chopped)
- Olive oil (1 tsp.)
- Zucchini (2 sliced)
- Mushrooms (1 cup)
- Carrots (3 chopped)
- Tomato paste (2 cups)
- Canned tomatoes (1 can)
- Stock cube (1)
- Herbs
- Vegan Mince
- Gravy powder (1 package)

What to do:
Boil, peel and mash some potatoes with a little salt and some vegan margarine. Sauté onions with some olive oil in a saucepan until tender and to this add chopped zucchini, mushrooms, and carrots. After the veggies have softened add tomato paste, canned tomatoes, stock cube, herbs and casserole mince and stir well. Make thick gravy with gravy powder and some water and pour into this veggie mix. Cool for about 25-30 minutes. In a baking tray, pour this veggie mixture and layer the mashed potato mix on top. Bake this dish for around 25-30 minutes or until the top is nicely browned.

Day 8

"The future depends on what we do in the present."

- *Gandhi*

5-ingredient healthy delicious smoothie for breakfast –

What you need:
- Mixed berries (1 cup, frozen)
- Spinach (2 handfuls, fresh)
- Mixed fruit juice (2-3 cups)
- Banana (1 frozen)
- Flaxseed (1/4 cup)

What to do:
In a blender, blitz together frozen berry mix, spinach, flaxseed, mixed fruit juice, and a frozen banana and your delicious breakfast smoothie is ready.

Peking Mock "duck" pancakes for lunch –

What you need:
- Vegan "duck" (12 oz.)
- Duck sauce (5 tsp.)
- Vegan pancake batter (1 prepackaged)
- Onions (1 shredded)
- Cucumber (1 thinly sliced)

What to do:
Thaw the mock duck and put into a baking dish. Slather it with Peking duck sauce and bake for about 30 minutes at 200C. Shred the baked mock duck. Use ready made vegan pancake batter and cook the pancakes as directed. To serve, take a pancake, layer with Peking duck sauce, add shredded onions, cucumbers, and the mock duck and roll it gently. Your savory pancake is ready to enjoy.

Eggplant and Tomato Pasta for Dinner –

What to use:
- Olive Oil (2 tsp.)
- Onions (1 sliced)

- Garlic (2 bulbs, minced)
- Eggplant (1 chopped)
- Balsamic vinegar (2 tsp.)
- Tomatoes (1 canned)
- Tomato Paste (1 can)
- Herbs
- Sun-dried tomatoes (1 cup)
- Chili Flakes (1 ½ tsp.)
- Sugar (1 tsp.)
- Water (2 cups)

What to do:
In a large pan, add olive oil and sauté onions and minced garlic cloves. Add chopped eggplant and balsamic vinegar and cook until the veggies are soft and tender. Now add canned tomatoes, tomato paste, dried herbs, sun-dried tomatoes, chili flakes (if you like, add spice), sugar and some water. Bring this mixture to a full boil and cook it down for about half an hour. Cook the pasta separately and drain the excess water. Add the cooked pasta to the cooked veggie mixture and mix well. Add basil for improved flavor, to taste.

Chapter 4: Meal Plan and Outline Recipes for Block II

Day 9

"Vegan food is soul food in its truest form. Soul food means to feed the soul. And to me, your soul is your intent. If your intent is pure, you are pure."

- *Erykah Bad*

Blueberry maple and protein shake for breakfast –

What to use:
- Low-fat yogurt (3 cups)
- Vanilla protein powder (1 scoop)
- Blueberries (frozen, ½ cup)
- Maple extract (2 tsp.)
- Flaxseed (1/3 cup)
- Ice

What to do:
In a blender, mix low-fat yogurt, 1 scoop of vanilla protein powder, ½ cup blueberries (frozen), maple extract (to taste), flaxseed meal, and some ice cubes. Your delicious and nutritious breakfast shake is ready

Veggie fritters for lunch –

What to use:
- All-purpose flour (2 cups)
- Soy milk (2/3 cup)
- Choice of vegetables (1/2 cup)
- Salt (1 tbsp.)
- Pepper (1 tbsp.)
- Oil (1 tsp.)

What to do:
Mix all-purpose flour and soy milk to form batter for the fritters. Stir in sliced vegetables of your choice (zucchini, carrots, potatoes, broccoli florets, onions) and

season with salt and pepper. Heat a little oil in a large skillet and spoon out a little of this mixture at a time giving it a round flat shape. Flip over and cook the other side after one side is cooked. Remove from heat, drain excess oil on tissue paper and serve hot.

Saucy tofu skewers for dinner – Cut out tofu and all your favorite veggies in roughly the same size squares. Place them on a bamboo or metal skewer. Cover with any of your favorite vegan sauces and leave to marinate for some time Barbecue or grill on a skillet until cooked. Serve with extra sauce.

Day 10

"Nothing will benefit human health and increase the chances for survival of life on Earth as much as the evolution to a vegetarian diet."
— Albert Einstein

Kale-based smoothie for breakfast –

What to use:
- Banana (1 whole)
- Mixed berries (frozen, ½ cup)
- Hemp seeds (1 tbsp)
- Kale (2 cups)
- Pomegranate juice (⅔ cup)
- Water

What to do:
In a food blender, blitz together 1 banana (medium ripe), ½ cup mixed berries (frozen), 1 tbsp. hulled hemp seeds, 2 cups kale leaves (fresh or frozen), 2/3 cup pomegranate juice, and some water (depending on the consistency you like; less water if you want a thick smoothie and more water if you want a thin smoothie).

Parsnip and Tempeh Rolls for lunch –

What to use:
- Garlic (1 bulb, minced)
- Onions (1 diced)
- Oil (2 tsp.)
- Cumin (1 tbsp.)
- Sage (1 ½ oz.)
- Marjoram (2 oz.)
- Thyme (1 oz.)
- Salt (1 tbsp.)
- Pepper (1 tbsp.)
- Parsnip (2 chopped)
- Tempeh (6 oz.)
- Worcestershire sauce (anchovy free)

- Water
- Soy sauce (2 tsp.)
- Phyllo pastry sheets

What to do:
Fry garlic and onions in a little oil until soft and add spices including cumin powder, dried sage, marjoram, thyme, salt and pepper and cook until the aromas are released. Add grated parsnip and tempeh to this mixture until soft. Add anchovy-free Worcestershire sauce, water, and soy sauce and cook (stirring continuously) for 4-5 minutes more until the parsnips are fully cooked. Season with salt and pepper and keep aside.

Cut pastry sheets such that you can make rectangle rolls. Spread the tempeh and parsnip filling over the pastry, then fold over the pastry sheet and press the meeting ends together to seal well. Then cut these filled portions into bite-sized pieces. Bake them in a preheated oven at 180C for about 15 minutes or until they are golden brown.

Chili non-carne for dinner -

What to use:
- Onions (1 chopped)
- Garlic (2 bulbs, minced)
- Zucchini (1 sliced)
- Carrots (2 sliced)
- Mushrooms (1 cup)
- Capsicum (1 tbsp.)
- Cumin (2 tbsp.)
- Coriander (1 tbsp.)
- Fennel seeds (2 tsp.)
- Chili flakes (1 tsp.)
- Peppercorns (1 tbsp.)
- Paprika (1 tbsp.)
- Canned Tomatoes (1 can)
- Tomato Paste (1 can)
- Kidney beans (3 cups)
- Stock cube

What to do:
In a big saucepan, fry onions and garlic until soft. Add zucchini, carrots,

mushrooms, and capsicum and fry some more until veggies are all tender. Add a spice mixture consisting of cumin powder, coriander powder, fennel seeds, chili flakes, peppercorns, paprika, and salt. Cook for some more time until the spices release aroma. To this add canned tomatoes, tomato paste, kidney beans (canned) and stock cube. Simmer for about half an hour and your non-carne is ready. Serve with rice, baked potatoes, enchiladas, or tacos.

Day 11

"Raw food is the best way to have the cleanest energy. We take so much care about what kind of fuel we put in our car, what kind of oil. We care about that sometimes more than the fuel that we're looking at putting in our bodies. It's cleaner burning fuel."
- *Woody Harrelson*

Mango Green Smoothie for breakfast–

What to use:
- Mango (frozen, 1 ½ cups)
- Strawberries (frozen, 1 cup)
- Spinach (1 cup, fresh)
- Almond milk (1 cup)
- Sweetener

What to do:
In a blender, blitz together 1 ½ cups of frozen mango, 1 cup frozen strawberries, 1 cup spinach (fresh), 1 cup almond milk, and a vegan sweetener like stevia or agave. Your mango green smoothie is ready.

Spicy Couscous for lunch –

What to use:
- Olive oil (2 tsp.)
- Onions (1/2 chopped)
- Garlic (1 bulb, minced)
- Capsicum (1 chopped)
- Zucchini (1 sliced)
- Cumin (1 tsp.)
- Coriander (1 tsp.)
- Pepper (1 tbsp.)
- Fennel (1 tbsp.)
- Chili flakes (1 tbsp.)
- Salt (1 tbsp.)
- Couscous (2 cups)
- Water (boiling)
- Chickpeas (cooked)

- Stock powder (1 package)
- Sun-dried tomatoes (2/3 cup)

What to do:
In a large pan, heat some olive oil and sauté onions and garlic until translucent. Add capsicum and zucchini and cook until soft. Add spice mixture consisting of cumin, coriander, black pepper, fennel, chili flakes, and salt. Fry for another minute until the aromas of the spices are released. Stir in some couscous and add boiling water and some stock powder into this veggie mixture. Now add some sun-dried tomatoes and cooked chickpeas to this and mix thoroughly. Cover the pan with a lid and put off the heat and let it be for about 5 minutes. Once the couscous has absorbed all the stock, sprinkle some freshly chopped coriander and your lunch is ready.

Thai Red Curry for Dinner –

What to use:
- Onions (1 chopped)
- Red curry paste (2 tsp.)
- Coconut milk (1 cup)
- Vegetable stock (2 cups)
- Tofu (8 oz.)
- Mushrooms (1 cup)
- Sugar (2 tsp.)
- Soy sauce (1 tsp.)
- Capsicum (1 chopped)
- Bamboo shoots (1/3 cup)
- Chili (2 tsp.)
- Sugar snap peas (2 cups)

What to do:
Fry onions in a little bit of oil until tender. To this add 2 tbsp. of red curry paste (ensure that the paste has no shrimp paste in it). Stir for a while and then slowly add coconut milk in small amounts stirring continuously. Now add vegetable stock. Bring this mixture to a boil and then reduce the heat to allow it to simmer.

Add tofu, mushroom, sugar, soy sauce, and capsicum to this mixture and continue to simmer for 10 more minutes. Now add bamboo shoots, chili, and sugar snap peas and cook for another 5 minutes. Serve with steamed rice.

Day 12

"Strive for progress, not perfection."

- *Unknown*

Mango-Strawberry with lime smoothie for breakfast –

What to use:
- Mangoes (2, cubed)
- Strawberries (frozen, ½ cup)
- Lime juice (half lime)
- Ice

What to do:
In a blender, blitz together 2 mangoes (cubed), ½ a cup frozen strawberries, lime juice (from half a lime), and ice cubes. Your lime mango-strawberry smoothie is ready.

Asparagus and Pine Nut Tart for lunch –

What to use:
- Pastry sheet
- Mustard (1/2 tsp.)
- Asparagus (5 pieces)
- Vegan cream cheese (1 tsp.)
- Non-dairy milk (1 tbsp)
- Vegan cheese (to taste)
- Pine nuts (1/3 cup)

What to do:
Cut a sheet of pastry into two such as that you have 2 equal rectangles. At ½ cm from the edge, gently score the 4 sides of the pastry. Spread some mustard on the pastry sheet and place 5 asparagus sticks on each of the two rectangles (within the scored line). Bake until the pastry starts to rise. Mix together vegan cream cheese and 1 tbsp. non-dairy milk. Pour this mixture over the pastry and sprinkle some vegan cheese over. Put the pastry in the oven again and bake for about 10 minutes until golden brown. Remove from the oven and sprinkle roasted pine nuts over the tarts. Enjoy.

Tacos and Guacamole for dinner –

What to use:
- Prepared chili non-carne
- Taco size toruntilas
- Salad leaf mixture
- Gucamole
- Salsa

What to do:
First make the chili non-carne (recipe described in Day 10 dinner meal). First, heat the soft taco shells on a skillet and then fill them with salad leaves, guacamole, salsa, and chili non-carne. Your simple yet delicious taco meal is ready.

Day 13

"Strength does not come from physical capacity. It comes from an indomitable will."
- *Mahatma Gandhi*

Jelly Dates and Peanut butter smoothie for breakfast –

What to use:
- Medjool dates (4)
- Peanut butter (1 tbsp)
- Banana (1 frozen)
- Almond milk (¾ cup)
- Blueberries (frozen, 1/3 cup)
- Flaxseed (1 tbsp)

What to do:
In a blender, blitz together 4 medjool dates, 1 tbsp. peanut butter, 1 frozen banana, ¾ cup almond milk, 1/3 cup frozen blueberries, and 1 tbsp. flaxseed meal. Blend until desired smooth consistency. Your jelly dates and peanut butter smoothie is ready for enjoyment.

Pumpkin soup for lunch –

What to use:
- Oil
- Onions (1 chopped)
- Pumpkin squash (2 chunked)
- Water (boiling)
- Noodle soup packet (1 packaged)
- Salt (1 tsp.)
- Pepper (1 tsp.)

What to do:
In a large pan, heat up some oil and sauté onions and pumpkin squash chunks until they start to brown. Pour boiling water until the veggies are completely covered and then stir in 1 packet of noodle soup. Simmer the pan contents until the pumpkin squash is cooked through. Blend this entire mixture and season with salt and pepper. Serve with some crusty bread.

Marinated Tempeh Steak with Veggies for dinner –

What to use:
- Tempeh (4 blocks)
- Garlic (1 bulb, minced)
- Soy sauce (2 tsp.)
- Oil (2 tsp.)
- Pine nuts (1/3 cup)
- Asparagus (6 oz.)
- Baby potatoes (2 cups)
- Vegan margarine
- Parsley (1/3 cup)

What to do:
Slice the tempeh block into two thinner pieces and then cut these again so that you get 4 blocks of tempeh all together. Marinate these tempeh blocks with garlic-infused soy sauce for as long as you can. Drizzle some oil in a skillet and fry the marinated tempeh until both the sides are brown.

For the veggies, roast pine nuts and steam the asparagus spears. Steam baby potatoes until they are soft. Toss the boiled potatoes with some vegan margarine in a hot skillet and chopped parsley. Plate the tempeh and arrange all the veggies on the side.

Day 14

"Energy and persistence conquer all things."
- *Benjamin Franklin*

Berry, Banana, and Sesame Smoothie for breakfast –

What to use:
- Banana (1 whole)
- Wheat germ (4 tbsp.)
- Sesame seeds (4 tbsp)
- Strawberries (fresh, 5)
- Yogurt (berry flavored, 2 tbsp)

What to do:
Put 1 small banana, 1 tbsp. wheat germ, 4 tbsp. of sesame seeds, 5 strawberries, and 2 tbsp. of berry-flavored yogurt and blend until smooth. Pour into a glass and have a wholesome vegan breakfast.

Tempeh strips with salad wraps for lunch –

What to use:
- Tempeh (12 oz.)
- Garlic (2 bulbs, minced)
- Canola oil (1 tbsp.)
- Sesame oil (1 tsp.)
- Vegan margarine (1 tsp.)
- Beetroot dip (3 tsp.)
- Wrap
- Fresh veggies of choice

What to do:
Marinate tempeh with a garlic infused mixture of canola and sesame oils. After marination cut into strips and cook in a hot skillet until both sides are brown. Spread vegan margarine and beetroot dip on the ready-to-eat wraps and fill the wraps with tempeh strips and your veggies (cut into strips).

Lentil Dahl for dinner –

What to use:
- Garlic (1 bulb, minced)
- Onion (1 chopped)
- Vegetable oil (2 tsp.)
- Cumin (1 tbsp.)
- Ginger (2 tbsp. grated)
- Turmeric (1 tbsp.)
- Garam masala (1 tbsp.)
- Lentils (2 cups)
- Cardamom pods
- Stock powder
- Cinnamon (1 tbsp.)
- Bay leaves

What to do:
In a saucepan, fry garlic and onions in a little bit of vegetable oil until onions are translucent. Add cumin, ginger, turmeric powder, and garam masala powder and continue to fry until the aromas of the spices are released. Now add some water, lentils, cardamom pods, stock powder, cinnamon powder, and bay leaves. Cook, while stirring occasionally, for about 25 minutes until the mixture is fully cooked. Serve hot with rice or your favorite crusty bread.

You are halfway done!

Congratulations on making it to the halfway point of the journey. Many try and give up long before even getting to this point, so you are to be congratulated on this. You have shown that you are serious about getting better every day. I am also serious about improving my life, and helping others get better along the way. To do this I need your feedback. Click on the link below and take a moment to let me know how this book has helped you. If you feel there is something missing or something you would like to see differently, I would love to know about it. I want to ensure that as you and I improve, this book continues to improve as well. Thank you for taking the time to ensure that we are all getting the most from each other.

http://viewbook.at/veganbook

Day 15

"Ability is what you're capable of doing. Motivation determines what you do. Attitude determines how well you do it."
- *Lou Holtz*

Cheesecake strawberry smoothie for breakfast –

What to use:
- Strawberries (1 cup)
- Oil
- Vegan Cottage cheese (1 cup)
- Chia seeds (1/3 cup)
- Sweetener
- Ice

What to do:
First roast the strawberries with any vegetable oil and bake for about 20 minutes until the juices of the berries are released. Now, in a blender, blitz together cottage cheese, roasted strawberries, chia seeds, a sweetener like an agave or stevia, and ice cubes. Pour the smoothie into a glass and enjoy your breakfast.

Vegetable burger and raw salad for lunch –

What to use:

- Prepared vegetable or bean burger patty
- Fresh vegetables and leafy greens
- Lime juice (to taste)
- Agave (to taste)

What to do:
Heat up a ready-to-eat vegetable or red lentil burger until brown on both sides. Chop up some favorite vegetables like cucumber, tomatoes, cabbage, and baby spinach and make a salad with a simple lime juice and agave dressing. Enjoy your lunch of vegetable burger and salad.

Roast with cooked Vegetables for dinner –

What to use:
- Potatoes (2 diced)
- Butternut squash (1 diced)
- Zucchini (2 chopped)
- Carrots (3 chopped)
- Corn
- Onions (1 chopped)
- Garlic (2 bulbs minced)
- Rosemary
- Capsicum (3 chopped)
- Vegan roast

What to do:
In a greased baking pan, place potatoes, butternut squash, zucchini, carrots, corn, onions, and garlic and sprinkle some rosemary over. Cover the pan with aluminum foil and bake at 180C in a preheated oven for about 30 minutes. Remove the vegan roast from the packet and rub with olive oil, rosemary, and mint. Once the veggies have cooked for 30 minutes, place the roast in the middle, add some capsicum and bake for another half hour. Serve with garlic bread and a mushroom gravy.

Day 16

"Motivation is what gets you started. Habit is what keeps you going."
- *Jim Ryan*

Raspberry-banana smoothie for breakfast –

What to use:
- Banana (1 frozen)
- Raspberries (frozen, 1 ¼ cup)
- Orange juice (¾ cup)
- Pomegranate juice (½ cup)
- Almond milk (unsweetened, ¾ cup)

What to do:
In a food processor, blend together 1 large, ripe banana (frozen), 1 ¼ cup raspberry (frozen), ¾ cup orange juice, ½ cup pomegranate juice, and ¾ cup unsweetened almond milk. Your raspberry-banana smoothie is ready.

Sweet corn and cauliflower soup for lunch –

What to use:
- Cauliflower head (1)
- Corn on cob (2)
- Potato (1 large, diced)
- Leek (1)
- Vegetable stock (1 cup)
- Salt (1 tbsp.)
- Pepper (1 tbsp.(
- Water (2 cups)

What to do:
In a big saucepan, put a ½ head of cauliflower (cut into florets), kernels from 2 corn cobs, 1 large potato (diced), 1 small leek, 1 cup of vegetable stock, salt, and pepper and one liter of water. Bring this mixture to a boil and then simmer on a low flame for about 15-20 minutes until veggies are cooked through. Cool and then blend in a food processor. Serve hot with crusty bread.

Spaghetti Bolognese for dinner –

What to use:
- Onions (1/2 chopped)
- Garlic (1 bulb minced)
- Mushrooms (1 cup)
- Zucchini (1 sliced)
- Carrots (2 chopped)
- Tomatoes (canned)
- Worcestershire sauce (2 tsp. anchovy free)
- Tomato paste (1 can)
- Stock cube
- Herbs
- Spaghetti (1 box)

What to do:
In a large saucepan, fry onions and garlic with some oil until soft. Now add mushrooms, zucchini, and carrots, stir gently and cook for 2-3 minutes. Now add canned tomatoes, anchovy-free Worcestershire sauce, tomato paste, stock cube, and herbs and mix well. Season the mixture with salt and pepper. Simmer for about 20 minutes. Cook and drain spaghetti as directed on the packet and serve with the sauce.

Chapter 5: Meal Plan and Recipes for Block III

"Clear your mind of can't."
- *Samuel Johnson*

Day 17

Peach Oat Smoothie for breakfast –

What to use:
- Peaches (2 cubed)
- Chia seeds (1 tbsp)
- Banana (1/2)
- Uncooked oats (¼ cup)
- Almond milk (unsweetened, ½ cup)
- Orange juice ¼ cup
- Agave (optional)

What to do:
In a blender, blitz together 2 ripe peaches (cut into cubes), 1 tbsp. chia seeds, ½ frozen banana, ¼ cup uncooked oats, ½ cup almond milk (unsweetened), ¼ orange juice, and agave (if you want). Your peach oat smoothie is done.

Stir Fry Veggies and Tempeh with rice for lunch –

What to use:
- Oil (1 tsp.)
- Stir fry vegetables (2 cups)
- Choice of spices
- Tempeh (1 ½ cups)
- Soy sauce (2 tsp.)
- Sweet chili sauce (1 tsp.)

What to do:
Place some oil in a large pan and stir fry vegetables of your choice such as broccoli florets, carrots, zucchini, mushrooms, onions, and whatever else you like to stir fry. Add spices like curry powder, cumin powder, and coriander powder and continue to stir fry until all veggies are tender. Add some tempeh (cut into squares) and then add a mixture of soy sauce and sweet chili sauce. Toss everything together and

serve on a plate of steamed hot rice.

Soy strips Rougaille with a watercress salad for dinner –

What to use:
- Olive Oil (2 tsp.)
- Onions (1 chopped)
- Garlic (1 bulb minced)
- Thyme
- Ginger (1 oz.)
- Tomato paste (1 can)
- Tomatoes (1 diced)
- Chili (1 tsp.)
- Soy strips (1 package)
- Watercress (3 oz.)
- Carrots (2 chopped)
- Capsicum (2 chopped)
- Orange juice (1/3 cup)
- Salt (1 tbsp.)
- Pepper (1 tbsp.

What to do:
In a large pan, heat some oil and sauté onions, garlic, thyme, and some ginger. Add tomato paste, tomatoes, and some chili and let it simmer for 2 minutes. In another pan, fry marinated soy strips in olive oil until brown. To the simmering sauce add the fried soy strips with some water and bring to a boil. Then reduce the heat and allow it to simmer for about 10 minutes or until the sauce thickens. For the watercress salad, toss together chopped watercress, carrots, and capsicum along with vinaigrette of orange juice, salt, and pepper. Place the salad on a plate and over this place the sauce-filled soy strips. Enjoy your dinner

Day 18

"Our greatest weakness lies in giving up. The most certain way to succeed is always to try just one more time."

- *Thomas Edison*

Banana bread smoothie for breakfast –

What to use:
- Banana (1 frozen)
- Quinoa (cooked, ½ cup)
- Walnuts (1 tbsp)
- Flaxseed (2 tbsp)
- Date (1)
- Cinnamon (¾ tsp)
- Ice

What to do:
Place 1 frozen banana, ½ cup quinoa (cooked), 1 tbsp. walnuts. 2 tbsp. flaxseed, 1 medjool date, ¾ tsp cinnamon powder, and some ice cubes. Blitz together, pour into your glass and enjoy your smoothie.

Crispy Mock Chicken with Potato Mash for lunch –

What to use:
- Mock chicken breast (1 prepackaged)
- Oil
- Mashed Potatoes (4 potatoes, mashed)

What to do:
Cut "mock" chicken into chunks or strips and put them into a Ziploc pouch along with seasoning and breadcrumbs for about 30 minutes. Heat some oil in a pan, and fry this in batches until golden brown. Serve on a plate of hot mashed potatoes.

Avocado on Toast for dinner –

What to use:
- Bread

- Vegan margarine
- Avocados (2 whole)
- Fresh veggies (optional)

What to do:
Take a slice of your favorite bread and toast with some vegan margarine until golden brown. Pile mashed avocados over this and enjoy a healthy and extremely easy-to-make vegan meal. You could add some sprouts and raw veggies for some crunch and extra energy.

Day 19

"Setting goals is the first step in turning the invisible into the visible."

- *Tony Robbins*

Green Apple and Cucumber Smoothie for breakfast –

What to use:
- Green apple (1 chopped)
- Walnuts (1 tbsp)
- Cucumber (1/2)
- Avocado (1/4)
- Agave (optional)
- Ice

What to do:
In a blender, blitz together chopped green apple, 1 tbsp. walnuts, ½ a cucumber, ¼ of an avocado (chopped), some agave (if you want), and ice cubes. Your delicious green apple and cucumber smoothie is ready.

Enchiladas and Guacamole for lunch –

What to use:
- Prepared chili non-carne
- Toruntilas (1 package)
- Salsa (4 oz.)
- Guacamole (6 oz.)

What to do:
First make some chili non-carne as described in an earlier meal plan day (specifically Day 10's dinner recipe). Get yourself some ready made toruntilas and salsa, or create your own salsa by running onions, tomatoes, garlic, jalapenos or chili of choice, lime juice and fresh cilantro through a food processor. On a toruntila, spread some chili non-carne, and fold it over. Bake until the toruntilas are slightly brown. Remove from the oven and place some salsa on top. Serve hot with some fresh guacamole.

Bombay potatoes with pita bread for dinner –

What to use:
- Bombay potato packet (1 prepackaged)
- Pita bread
- Vegan sour cream (3 oz.)
- Coriander (1 oz.)

What to do:
Heat the packet of Bombay potatoes and cook as directed. Warm the pita bread and spread the potatoes in a layer on the top. Garnish the pita with some vegan sour cream and some fresh coriander. Dig right in.

Day 20

"I attribute my success to this: I never gave or took any excuse."

- *Florence Nightengale*

Strawberries smoothie for breakfast –

What to use:
- Strawberries (frozen, 1 cup)
- Chia seeds (1/3 cup)
- Flaxseed (1/3 cup)
- Oats (2/3 cup)
- Apple cider vinegar (2 tsp.)
- Vanilla extract (2 tbsp.)
- Ice

What to do:
Place 1 cup frozen strawberries, some chia seeds, some flaxseed, raw oats, apple cider vinegar, vanilla extract, and some ice cubes. Blitz all together with blender and your smoothie is ready.

Roasted vegetable lasagna for lunch –

What to use:
- Eggplant (1 chopped)
- Capsicum (2 chopped)
- Zucchini (1 chopped)
- Onions (1 chopped)
- Olive oil (2 tsp.)
- Salt (1 tbsp.)
- Pepper (1 tbsp.)
- Pesto
- Tomatoes (2 diced)
- Tomato paste (1 can)
- Vegan margarine
- Flour (2/3 cup)
- Vegan cream cheese (1/3 cup)
- Lasagna noodles (1 package)

What to do:
In a baking dish, put together chopped eggplant, capsicum, zucchini, and onions. Drizzle some olive oil and season vegetable mixture with salt and pepper. Toss it all together and bake in a medium heated oven until tender. Once this is cooled, add pesto, chopped tomatoes, and tomato paste and mix thoroughly.

Make a white sauce with vegan margarine, flour, and vegan cream cheese. Now, take a baking dish, make a vegetable layer at the bottom; next place a lasagna sheet, and then pour the white sauce over. Repeat this layering process until the ingredients are all used up. Bake for about 30-40 minutes until the top is lightly brown. Enjoy your vegan lasagna hot.

One-pot Black Bean Chili for dinner-

What to use:
- Carrots (2 chopped)
- Peppers (2 chopped)
- Onion (1 chopped)
- Diced tomatoes (1 diced)
- Cumin (1 tsp.)
- Garlic (1 bulb, minced)
- Paprika (1 tsp.)
- Chili powder (1 tsp.)
- Black beans (1 ½ cups)
- Corn (1 cup, frozen)
- Vegan cheese (optional)

What to do:
In a large pan sauté carrots, peppers and onion until tender. After sautéed add diced tomatoes and seasonings such as cumin, garlic, paprika and chili powder. Mix these ingredients well and add in black beans and corn kernels. Let simmer a while before eating for spices to fully blend flavors. Distribute to a bowl and top with vegan cheese, served most deliciously with crusty bread or a baked potato.

Day 21

"Outstanding people have one thing in common: An absolute sense of mission."

- *Zig Ziglar*

Green Smoothie for breakfast –

What to use:
- Cucumber (1)
- Spinach (3 cups, raw)
- Melon (2 cups)
- Green tea (1 cup)
- Lemon juice (1 tsp.)
- Agave (optional)
- Ice

What to do:
Blend together 1 cucumber (diced), 3 cups of spinach (raw), 2 cups melon (cubed), some brewed green tea, a little lemon juice (for tartness), some agave (if you want), and some ice cubes. Once nicely blended pour into a glass and enjoy your breakfast.

Stir-fry vegetables with marinated soy strips for lunch –

What to use:
- Oil
- Favorite vegetables
- Soy strips (marinated)
- Seasonings and sauce of choice

What to do:
In a large pan, with a little oil, stir-fry all your favorite veggies along with some marinated soy strips. Add spices and sauces of your choice. Serve on a plate of hot steamed rice.

Vegan hot dogs for dinner –

What to use:
- Vegan hot dogs (2)

- Vegan margarine
- Bun (2)
- Mustard (to taste)
- Cucumber (1/2 thinly sliced)
- Tomato (1/2 thinly sliced)
- Lettuce (a few leaves)

What to do:
Cook the ready made vegan hot dogs by boiling, steaming, or frying. Spread vegan margarine on one side of the bun (cut in half), smear mustard on the other half, place the hot dogs in the middle, and pile on cucumbers and tomato slices and some lettuce leaves. Bring the two halves of the bun together and your dinner is ready.

Day 22

"Nothing is impossible; the word itself says 'I'm possible!'"

- Audrey Hepburn

Mint and chocolate chip smoothie for breakfast –

What to use:
- Peppermint tea (1 cup)
- Almond milk (1 cup, unsweetened)
- Banana (1 frozen)
- Spinach (2 cups, fresh)
- Hemp seeds (1 tsp)
- Chocolate chips (1/3 cup)
- Ice

What to do:
Place a peppermint tea in boiling water and get a nicely concentrated cup of peppermint tea ready. In a blender, put together 1 cup unsweetened almond milk, 1 frozen banana, 2 cups of spinach, 1 tsp of hemp seeds, 2 tbsp. of chocolate chips, and ice cubes. Blitz everything and pour into a glass. Put some more chocolate chips on top and your breakfast is ready.

Thai noodles for lunch –

What to use:
- Vermicelli noodles (1 package)
- Olive oil
- Chopped stir fry vegetables of choice (2 cups)
- Soy sauce (1 tsp.)
- Sesame oil (1 tsp.)

What to do:
Cook vermicelli noodles as directed on the packet. Drain and keep aside. Heat some olive oil in a large pan and add chopped veggies like celery, bok choy, spring onions, mushrooms, peanuts, chili, ginger, and garlic. Cook until the vegetables are tender. Make a mixture of light soy sauce and sesame oil. Once the vegetables are nicely tender, stir in the noodles and add the sauce mixture. Mix well. Remove

from heat and serve hot.

Sandwich with soy strips for dinner –

What to use:
- Bread
- Marinated soy strips (1 package)
- Raw vegetables of choice (sliced)
- Vegan margarine
- Dijon mustard (to taste)

What to do:
Make a yummy sandwich with your favorite bread slices and marinated soy strips. Add some raw vegetables for some crunch. You can use vegan margarine and Dijon mustard as sandwich spreads and dig right in.

Day 23

"The successful warrior is the average man, with laser-like focus."

- *Bruce Lee*

Apple Smoothie for breakfast –

What to use:
- Apple (1)
- Cherries (½ cup, pitted)
- Cucumber (1/2)
- Raspberries (½ cup)
- Chia seeds (1 tsp)
- Ice

What to do:
Blitz together 1 apple, ½ cup cherries, ½ cucumber, ½ cup raspberries, 1 tsp chia seeds, and some ice cubes. Pour into your favorite glass and enjoy the apple smoothie.

Borscht for lunch –

What to use:
- Beetroots (4)
- Oil
- Celery (3 stalks, chopped)
- Carrots (2 chopped)
- Mushrooms (1 cup)
- Leeks (3)
- Water

What to do:
Cook and peel beetroots. Grate half of it and thinly slice the remaining. In a large pan, heat oil, and add chopped celery, carrots, mushrooms, leeks and some water. Bring to a boil; add the grated beets, reduce the heat and simmer for about 10 minutes. In another pan, take some more water and boil the sliced beets and simmer on a medium heat for not more than 10 minutes. Drain out the beetroot slices (which you can discard) and pour the beetroot-infused juice into the other

simmering veggie mixture. Remove from heat. Season with spices of your choice and your yummy borscht is ready.

***Vegan prawns and some salad for dinner* –**
What to use:
- Mock prawns (prepackaged)
- Soy sauce (1 tsp.)
- Raw vegetables of choice (3 cups)
- Dressing or sauce of choice (to taste)

What to do:
In a hot skillet, fry the mock prawns with some oil. Sprinkle soy sauce over the mock prawn. Serve hot with crunchy veggies, tossed with dressing of choice.

Chapter 6: Meal Plan and Recipes for Block IV

Day 24

"Be miserable. Or motivate yourself. Whatever has to be done, it's always your choice."

- *Wayne Dyer*

Blueberries smoothie for breakfast –

What to use:
- Non-dairy milk (1 ½ cups)
- Oats (2 tbsp)
- Vanilla Protein powder (1 tsp)
- Vanilla extract
- Chia seeds (1 tsp)
- Blueberries (fresh, ½ cup)

What to do:
This needs a little bit of planning the night before. Combine 1 ½ cups of any non-dairy milk, 2 tbsp. of oats, 1 tsp of vanilla protein powder, a little vanilla extract and 1 tsp of chia seeds. Place in the fridge the night before. In the morning, blitz this mixture along with ½ cup blueberries and your smoothie is ready.

Tempeh Cottage Pie for lunch –

What to use:
- Cumin seeds (1 tsp.)
- Onion (1 chopped)
- Garlic (2 bulbs minced)
- Capers (2/3 cup)
- Tempeh (1 ½ cups)
- Carrots (2 chopped)
- Tomatoes (1 diced)
- Corn (1 cob)
- Peas (5 oz.)
- Sweet Potato (1)
- Water

- Tomato paste (1 can)
- Salt (1 tsp.)
- Pepper (2 tbsp.)
- Potatoes (2)
- Soy milk (1/3 cup)
- Vegan margarine

What to do:
Fry cumin seeds, onions, garlic, and capers until tender. Put in the tempeh and fry for a couple of minutes more. Add carrots, tomatoes, corn, peas, and sweet potato and cook for another 2-3 minutes. Add water and tomato paste; bring to a boil, reduce heat and simmer until the liquid reduces, but ensure that the mixture does not get too dry. Add salt and pepper for seasoning.

Nicely Mash par-boiled potatoes with soymilk and vegan margarine. Season this with salt and pepper. Pour the tempeh mixture onto a baking tray and evenly spread it out. Spread the mashed potato mixture over this layer and sprinkle paprika over the potatoes. Bake in a medium heated oven for 45 minutes until the potato layer is golden brown.

San Choy Bow for dinner –

What to use:
- Onion (1/2 chopped)
- Garlic (1 bulb minced)
- Ginger (1 root grated)
- Chili (1 tsp.)
- Mushrooms (1 cup)
- Vegan mince (1 package)
- Vegetable stock (1 cup)
- Coriander (1 tsp.)
- Soy sauce (2 tsp.)
- Lime juice (2 tbsp.)

What to do:
In a large wok, stir-fry onion, and garlic over a high heat. Add ginger, chili, and mushrooms and continue stir-frying for another 3 minutes. Mix in the vegan mince and stir-fry for some a few more minutes breaking down the lumps in the mince as you go along. Add stock and bring to a boil. Reduce heat and continue to simmer until the stock is fully absorbed. Stir in coriander, soy sauce, and some lime juice.

Serve hot on a platter of lettuce leaves.

Day 25

"I believe that the greatest gift you can give to the world and your family is a healthy you."
- *Joyce Meyer*

Raspberry lemon smoothie for breakfast –

What to use:
- Non-dairy milk (1 ½ cups)
- Raspberries (½ cup)
- Oats (2 tbsp)
- Lemon juice (1 tbsp)
- Chia seeds (1 tbsp)
- Almond butter (1 tbsp)
- Lemon zest
- Vanilla extract
- Stevia leaf powder

What to do:
This requires you to prepare the ingredients the night before. Combine 1 ½ cups of non-dairy milk, 1/2 cup of raspberry, 2 tbsp. oats, 1 tbsp. lemon juice, 1 tbsp. of chia seeds, 1 tbsp. of almond butter, a little lemon zest, vanilla extract, and stevia powder. Place in the fridge overnight. In the morning, blitz this mixture in a blender until smooth. Your smoothie is ready

Vegetable curry with rice for lunch –

What to use:
- *Vegetable oil*
- Onions (1 chopped)
- Cumin seeds (2 tsp.)
- Garlic (1 bulb minced)
- Potatoes (2)
- Cauliflower (1 head)
- Carrots (3 chopped)
- Mushrooms (1 ½ cups)
- French beans (2 cups)
- Peas (2 cups)

- Curry paste
- Turmeric (1 tsp.)
- Coriander (1 tsp.)
- Salt (2 tbsp.)
- Pepper (1 tbsp.)

What to do:
In a pan, heat some vegetable oil, and fry onions, garlic, and cumin seeds until onions are translucent. Add chopped vegetables including potatoes, cauliflower, carrots, mushrooms, French beans, and peas. Add curry paste, turmeric powder, and coriander powder. Sprinkle a little water and cook until the veggies are tender all the way through. Season the curry with salt and pepper. Serve hot on a layer of steamed rice.

Potato and vegetable salad for dinner –

What to use:
- Potatoes (3 steamed)
- Dijon mustard (1/3 cup)
- Vegan mayo (2/3 cup)
- Carrots (3 grated)
- Onions (1 chopped)

What to do:
Steam potatoes and keep aside. Make a sauce by mixing Dijon mustard and vegan mayonnaise. Cut the potatoes and stir in some grated carrots and finely chopped onions. Stir in the sauce. Mix thoroughly and your salad is ready to be polished off.

Day 26

"To keep the body in good health is a duty...otherwise we shall not be able to keep our mind strong and clear."

- *Buddha*

Blueberry peach smoothie for breakfast –

What to use:
- Peach (1/2)
- Blueberries (1 cup)
- Protein powder (1 scoop)
- Green tea (1 cup)
- Chia seeds (1 tsp)
- Probiotics
- Ice

What to do:
Blend together 1/2 a peach, 1 cup blueberries, 1 scoop protein powder, 1 cup prepared green tea, 1 tsp chia seeds, 1 serving probiotics, and some ice cubes in a blender until smooth. Enjoy your breakfast.

Stuffed tofu turkey for lunch –

What to use:
- Firm tofu (prepackaged)
- Tamari oil (1 tsp.)
- Olive oil (1 tsp.)
- Garlic (1 bulb crushed)
- Onions (1 chopped)
- Mushrooms (2 cups)
- Celery (4 stalks)
- Sesame oil (2 tsp.)
- Rosemary
- Thyme
- Sage
- Pepper (2 tbsp)
- Soy sauce (2 tsp.)

- Bread crumbs (prepackaged)

What to do:
You will need a large amount of firm tofu (about 2 kg). Crumble the firm tofu and add a marinade consisting of tamari oil, olive oil, and 2 cloves of crushed garlic. Stir well and keep aside. Tightly pack this tofu in a cheesecloth-lined colander and place cheesecloth over this too. Place a heavy object on top of this arrangement and let it rest for about an hour.

For the stuffing, fry onions, garlic, mushrooms, and celery in sesame oil. Add rosemary, thyme, dried sage, black pepper, and some soy sauce and cook until the vegetables are soft. Remove from heat. Add some breadcrumbs and mix well.

Remove the heavy object and the cheesecloth from the top of the tofu arrangement. Using a big ladle, scoop out tofu from the top such that about an inch of tofu is left on three sides. Press the stuffing into this hollow and put back the scooped tofu on top and press down firmly on all sides. Turn this over onto a greased baking dish and remove the other cheesecloth too. Bake the stuffed tofu for an hour until the top is nice and brown. Remove from the oven and cool. Your stuffed tofu is ready to be carved.

Zucchini fritters for dinner –

What to use:
- Zucchini (3)
- All-Purpose Flour (2/3 cup)
- Salt (1 tsp.)
- Pepper (2 tbsp.)
- Bread crumbs (1/3 cup)
- Herbs
- Oil

What to do:
Cut zucchini into baton shapes. Make a batter with all-purpose flour and season this with salt and pepper. Make a mixture of breadcrumbs and herbs. Dip the zucchini into the batter, then coat with the breadcrumb mixture and deep fry in hot oil. Serve hot with any sauce or chutney.

Day 27

"There's nothing more important than our good health- that's our principal capital asset."

- *Arlen Specter*

Pumpkin banana smoothie for breakfast –

What to use:
- Almond milk (1 cup)
- Banana (1/2)
- Pumpkin (canned, ½ cup)
- Maple syrup (½ tsp)
- Vanilla Extract
- Ginger (ground)
- All Spice
- Ice

What to do:
Blend together 1 cup almond milk, ½ banana, ½ cup canned pumpkin, ½ tsp maple syrup, vanilla extract, a little ground ginger, a pinch of all spice powder, and ice cubes in a food processor. When a thick, smooth consistency is reached, you can gulp down your smoothie.

Spanakopita for lunch –

What to use:
- Onions (1 chopped)
- Garlic (1 bulb minced)
- Spinach (2 cups, cooked, chopped)
- Mushroom (1 cup)
- Tofu (5 oz.)
- Pine nuts (1/3 cup, roasted)
- Salt (1 tbsp.)
- Pepper (1 tbsp.)
- Vegan margarine
- Phyllo dough (prepackaged)

What to do:
Make a filling with sautéed onions, garlic, cooked and chopped spinach, mushrooms, tofu, and some roasted pine nuts. Season the filling with salt and pepper. Use this filling to make rolls using readymade phyllo pastry dough. Place the rolls on a greased baking dish and brush them with melted margarine. Bake for about 15 minutes at 350 degrees or until golden brown. Serve warm with a vegan dip.

Vegan sushi for dinner –

What to use:
- Sushi rice (2 cups)
- Sugar (1 tbsp.)
- Rice vinegar (3 tsp.)
- Nori (seaweed sheet)
- Filling choice (optional)

What to do:
Cook rinsed sushi rice until the water is all absorbed. Stir in sugar and rice vinegar with the cooked rice and mix such that there are no lumps. Keep this aside. On a nori sheet, spread this rice evenly with enough space for any filling too. Other fillings to be considered may be avocado, carrots or cucumbers, julienned and placed to roll with the rice. Ensure you do not fill the nori wrapper too much, as then you would not be able to roll the sheets cleanly. Using a rolling mat, roll the sushi filled nori sheet and then remove the mat and cut into bite-sized pieces.

Day 28

"The foundation of success in life is good health: that is the substratum fortune; it is also the basis of happiness. A person cannot accumulate a fortune very well when he is sick."

- P. T. Barnum

Caramel apple green smoothie for breakfast –

What to use:
- Apple (1 diced, frozen)
- Almond milk (2 cups)
- Spinach (2 cups)
- Peanut butter (2 tbsp)
- Dates (2)
- Cinnamon
- Ice

What to do:
In a blender, put 1 frozen apple (diced), 1 cup almond milk, 2 cups spinach, 2 tbsp. peanut butter, 2 dates, ground cinnamon, and ice cubes and blitz together. Your smoothie is ready.

Asparagus and Mushroom Risotto for lunch –

What to use:
- Stock powder (prepackaged)
- Water
- Onion powder (1 tsp.)
- Mushrooms (1 cup)
- Dried herbs
- Vegan margarine
- Onions (1/2 chopped)
- Olive oil
- Rice (2/3 cup)
- Wine

- Vegetable stock (1 cup)

What to do:
In a large pan, mix water, stock powder, onion powder, mushrooms, and choice of dried herbs. Bring the pan to a boil and then reduce to a simmer. In another pan, melt vegan margarine with a little olive oil on a medium heat. Cook the onions until they are translucent and then add rice and stir continuously. To this rice, add wine and stir again. When the wine is completely gone, spoon in a ladle of vegetable stock. Now add the mushroom mixture. Keep adding stock as it continuously gets absorbed. Repeat this until you get the desired risotto consistency. Serve hot.

Mexican Beans and Baked Potato for dinner –

What to use:
- Potatoes (3)
- Mexican beans (3 cups)

What to do:
Poke potatoes through with fork and then place in a microwave for about 5 minutes, depending on size, so that it is not cooked through. Then cook in an oven until it is crisp on the outside and soft on the inside. Using pre-bought Mexican beans, heat up in sauce pan. If you would like to make homemade Mexican beans and have time for some extra prep, take pre-soaked pinto beans and season with sauteed garlic, onion and olive oil over medium heat. Add green chili, diced tomatoes, vegetable broth and then water until beans are covered. Bring to low boil, then allow to sit in simmer until beans are tender. Season with choice of seasonings to personal taste and stir, cooking for a few more minutes until flavors are absorbed. Place the beans over the cooked potatoes and enjoy your meal.

Day 29

"Food is really and truly the most effective medicine."
— Joel Fuhrman

Ultra Green smoothie for breakfast –

What to use:
- Spinach (2 cups)
- Coconut milk (unsweetened, 1 cup)
- Banana (1/2 frozen)
- Avocado (1/2 frozen)
- Hemp seeds (2 tsp)
- Ice

What to do:
In a food processor, place 2 cups spinach, 1 cup unsweetened coconut milk, ½ a frozen banana, ½ a frozen avocado, 2 tsp of hemp seeds, and ice cubes. Blitz all the ingredients together until you get a thick smoothie. Enjoy it.

Vegan pizza for lunch –

What to use:
- Vegan pizza crust (prepackaged)
- Vegan cheese (2 cups)
- Red capsicum (strips)
- Green capsicum (strips)
- Mushrooms (sliced)
- Olives

What to do:
Buy a ready-made vegan pizza crust base and layer it with vegan cheese, thin strips of red capsicum, green capsicum, sliced mushrooms, and olives over a layer of vegan pizza sauce, measured to taste. Bake for about 10-15 minutes.

Lentils, Leek, and Potato Soup for dinner –

What to use:

- Potatoes (2 chopped)
- Leeks (4)
- Red lentils (½ cup)
- Water
- Stock powder (prepackaged)
- Salt (1 tsp.)
- Pepper (2 tbsp.)

What to do:
Take chopped potatoes, leeks, and ½ cup of red lentils along with water and stock powder in a large pan. Bring it to a boil and then simmer on medium heat. Once cooked and cooled, blend in a food processor. Add a little hot water if you want a thinner consistency. Season the soup with salt and pepper.

Day 30

"The finish line is just the beginning of a whole new race."
- *Unknown*

Chocolate and Raspberry smoothie for breakfast –

What to use:
- Almond milk (1 cup)
- Spinach (2 cups)
- Raspberries (1 cup)
- Coconut (shredded, 2 tbsp)
- Cocoa powder (unsweetened, 1 tbsp)
- Ice

What to do:
Blend together 1 cup almond milk, 2 cups spinach, 1 cup raspberries, 2 tbsp. shredded coconut, 1 tbsp. cocoa powder, and some ice cubes in a food processor until you get a smooth consistency. Enjoy your smoothie.

Fried rice for lunch –

What to use:
- Onions (1/2 chopped)
- Fresh, chopped vegetables (2/3 cup)
- Soy sauce (2 tsp.)
- Sweet chili sauce (1 tsp.)
- Rice (2/3 cup)
- Salt (1 tsp.)
- Pepper (2 tbsp.)

What to do:
Heat oil in a large pan and sauté chopped onions. Add finely chopped veggies of your choice, with the recipe generally including cauliflower, French beans, peas, cabbage, and corn kernels. Add a sauce mixture of soy sauce and sweet chili sauce to this, measuring to taste, and cook until the veggies are tender. Add desired amount of cooked rice and toss and mix thoroughly. Season the fried rice with salt and pepper if needed. Serve hot.

Antipasto Pasta Salad for dinner –

What to use:
- Pasta (1 box)
- Capsicum (1)
- Onions (1/2 chopped)
- Carrots (2 chopped)
- Cucumber (1 sliced)
- Kalamata olives (1/3 cup)
- Balsamic vinegar (2 tsp.)
- Additional fresh vegetables

What to do:
Cook choice of pasta as per directions on the packet. Mix together thinly diced capsicum, onions, carrots, cucumber, and kalamata olives with some balsamic vinegar and choice of vegetables such as zucchini and tomato to create your antipasto salsa. Add the cooked pasta and toss all the ingredients together until pasta is well covered. Your salad is ready.

Conclusion – How to Stay Committed

If you are trying to change your lifestyle, it calls for immense commitment and hard work. It is quite easy to fall for loopholes and give up early or even halfway through because you cannot find the energy and motivation to handle the changes. This chapter is dedicated to helping you overcome these negative thoughts and help you stay committed to the vegan cause:

Set yourself easy to achieve targets initially – Setting unachievable targets can put you off as you see yourself as a failure. Take little at a time and be motivated by your small achievements. Slowly you will see setting higher targets and achieve them too.

Keep a journal and food tracker and make diligent notes – Write down everything. From what to eat, how much you have exercised, how difficult the day was in terms of keeping you on track, what were the motivation factors, what were the de-motivation factors, and more! Make note of everything no matter how trivial it may seem. When you are looking back, these notes will come in handy and will help you correct any mistakes.

Interact with people who are also facing these challenges – We are social animals and love the sense of belonging and a sense of identity. When we reach out to people who face the same situations that we face, we find that sense of belonging and the fear that we are the only ones with problems goes away. Moreover, when we interact with other people, ideas, and best practices can be exchanged which is good for all concerned.

Remember the process of change is always difficult and painful. But, if we do not take up these challenges we will stagnant which is the beginning of any end. You must steel yourself and work hard for a better tomorrow. When you are feeling low, think of the potential positive results of your endeavors and be motivated by those images and thoughts.

So, pick up the shovel, roll up your sleeves, take a firm stand, and start work immediately and be rest assured that you will find happiness, contentment and an amazing sense of achievement at the end of this seemingly arduous journey.

You're fully committed- what's next?

You made it through your 30 day course! It took a lot of discipline and willpower, but you made it like a champion and are now feeling better than ever. Your energy is high, your mind is clear and you are raring to go- and to continue on with a healthy Vegan lifestyle! So, what's the next step? This section is here to give you a few kick-start ideas on how to keep up with the Vegan diet and enhance the healthy new you even further.

Future Meal Planning
Maybe you want to go on with the Vegan diet but aren't sure where to start, or the set meal plan was really what kept you going. If you enjoyed the recipes and plans in this book, you can go ahead and rotate the meals again! Many of the recipes are customizable with different selections and cover enough days with different types of treats that you won't grow tiresome. If you're adventurous and want to try your hand at creating your own meal plan, start with a simple online search. Blogs and websites are plentiful with great ideas and recipes- your favorite vegan meal may be out there waiting at the tips of your fingers on the keyboard! Then, if you are the extreme adventurist, creating your own recipes might just be a fun new hobby! Now that you are familiar with common foods and structure of a healthy Vegan meal, take some of your favorite elements and flavors and see what you can come up with. You may end up with a couple of hit or miss concoctions, but it will be worth the experience and the chance at creating something awesomely new!

Share the excitement
Did you go on this 30 day challenge alone and just can't keep the excitement of vegan living to yourself any longer? Tell people about it and how much better you feel eating and living healthy! Testimonies go a long way as inspiration for people who are feeling miserable in their current ways. You could even get a circle of friends interested in vegan lifestyle and start a newsletter or a blog to keep yourself involved while giving your group updates on new tasty recipes, tips and motivation. Sometimes someone just needs a helping hand to get started, and your experience is just what they need! If no one you know seems too keen on the idea of Vegan eating, or if you're not sure you have quite the knowledge and gusto to start up an info group of any sort, search online for a Vegan-related forum or blog to follow yourself. You could earn support and knowledge while meeting new, like-minded people along the way. Win-win!

However you decide to keep involved and fully invested in your new Vegan lifestyle, just remember that that's what it is. A lifestyle that you chose for your health and your energy- an achievement to be proud of. Congratulations, and best regards!

Help me improve this book

While I have never met you, if you made it through this book I know that you are the kind of person that is wanting to get better and is willing to take on tough feedback to get to that point. You and I are cut from the same cloth in that respect. I am always looking to get better and I wish to not just improve myself, but also this book. If you have positive feedback, please take the time to leave a review. It will help other find this book and it can help change a life in the same way that it changed yours. If you have constructive feedback, please also leave a review. It will help me better understand what you, the reader, need to make significant improvements in your life. I will take your feedback and use it to improve this book so that it can become more powerful and beneficial to all those who encounter it.

http://viewbook.at/veganbook

REMEMBER TO JOIN THE GROUP NOW!

If you have not joined the Mastermind Self Development group yet, now is your time! You will receive videos and articles from top authorities in self development as well as a special group only offers on new books and training programs. There will also be a monthly member only draw that gives you a chance to win any book from your Kindle wish list!

If you sign up through this link http://www.mastermindselfdevelopment.com/specialreport you will also get a special free report on the Wheel of Life. This report will give you a visual look at your current life and then take you through a series of exercises that will help you plan what your perfect life looks like. The workbook does not end there; we then take you through a process to help you plan how to achieve that perfect life. The process is very powerful and has the potential to change your life forever. Join the group now and start to change your life!
http://www.mastermindselfdevelopment.com/specialreport

You will also love these other great titles from Mastermind Self Development!

You will want to check out these other great titles Mastermind Self Development. All available in the Kindle store or you can just click on covers below.

http://viewbook.at/selflove

http://mybook.to/positivethink

You can also find these titles by searching them in the Kindle store on Amazon.

Mindfulness

Beginners Guide on How to Shut Off
Your Brain and Stay in the Moment

Free membership into the Mastermind Self Development Group!

For a limited time, you can join the Mastermind Self Development Group for free! You will receive videos and articles from top authorities in self development as well as a special group only offers on new books and training programs. There will also be a monthly member only draw that gives you a chance to win any book from your Kindle wish list!

If you sign up through this link http://www.mastermindselfdevelopment.com/specialreport you will also get a special free report on the Wheel of Life. This report will give you a visual look at your current life and then take you through a series of exercises that will help you plan what your perfect life looks like. The workbook does not end there; we then take you through a process to help you plan how to achieve that perfect life. The process is very powerful and has the potential to change your life forever. Join the group now and start to change your life!
http://www.mastermindselfdevelopment.com/specialreport

Table of Contents

Introduction

Chapter 1: The Value of Mindfulness

Chapter 2: Creating the Calm

Chapter 3: Peace in Pandemonium

Chapter 4: The Practical Practice

Chapter 5: Maintaining Mindfulness

Conclusion

Introduction

Thank you and congratulations on purchasing this book! "*Mindfulness:* Beginners Guide on How to Shut Off Your Brain and Stay in the Moment" is a book written specifically for individuals who want to become more mindful, but who have a hard time encouraging their brain to be quiet. While you may feel as though mindfulness is not the technique for you, the truth is that everyone who has mastered mindfulness at one point or another had the exact same difficulty!

This book has been carefully crafted to bring resolutions for all who are struggling to achieve mindfulness in their lives. The wording and instructions are created in an easy-to-understand method that will allow you to understand the simplicity of being mindful, and how you can effortlessly draw it into your own life.

Mindfulness is a highly valuable tool that has the ability to achieve many things in a person's life. Whether you are seeking to add value to each day, eliminate the stress of worrying, or improve your quality of life, you can achieve all of that through mindfulness. In this book, you will be guided on how to achieve mindfulness on an average day, even if you are experiencing a particularly large amount of chaos or stress that may be causing you to feel extra edgy.

It is important to remember that mindfulness is a practice. Once you learn how to be mindful, you will have an easy time re-learning it. You will need to make sure you take the time each day to practice mindfulness, even when you become a master at it. Mindfulness is a balancing act where we are continually practicing our ability to stay in tune. Sometimes, you may notice that you have not been practicing mindfulness in your life. The result may show up as added stress, less mental involvement in day to day life, less clarity on what you are doing from moment to moment, and less quality of time spent with those around you. If you notice this is happening, the best thing you can do is become mindful of the existence of the chaos, and allow yourself to realign with a mindful state and start practicing your techniques again. In this book, you are going to learn exactly how you can do that.

Being mindful may feel difficult, especially for beginners. It is not natural in this day and age to tune out from the rest of the world and narrow in on what is happening in the moment. However, once you understand and implement this valuable technique in your life, you will notice that you feel your stress levels reduce significantly. You will also experience life greater, and with more joy. If you are ready to dive into learning about mindfulness, you are ready to begin chapter one.

Chapter 1: The Value of Mindfulness

Throughout history, a huge number of people have practiced mindfulness. As such, we see it across many religions and many other areas of culture. Mindfulness is a simple practice that, when practiced regularly, allows for humans to stay more focused on the specific task at hand, and resist the temptation to worry about or become absorbed in events of the past or the unpredictable future.

Mindfulness is a relatively simple task to learn once you understand exactly what it is and how you can use it in your daily life. This precious technique has the ability to add value to your life in many ways. Those who practice mindfulness on a regular basis notice increased happiness, greater synchronicity with themselves and the world around them, and even health improvements. Mindfulness truly is a valuable technique that has the ability to offer you a number of different benefits.

Emotional Benefits

Many people report a high number of emotional benefits that come from practicing mindfulness in their daily lives, and it makes sense as to why. Being mindful and staying present in the moment allows for people to experience the greatest benefit of each experience in life. Because of this heightened involvement in the experience, people report a greater result from it. The more involved they are in the moment, mentally, the more they understand about the moment and the more value they gain from it. This is because they are not renting any of their mind space out to unnecessary or irrelevant thoughts or emotions for the present moment. They are taking the time to notice every element of the experience, draw in all that it has to offer, and really take a heightened value from it. Because of this, people report feeling more peaceful, less stressed, happier, and a more genuine sense of joy that comes from being mindful.

Look at the below example to gain a greater understanding as to how mindfulness can change a situation:

Situation 1: *Sally was spending time with her Dad, as they often did on Fridays after school. He liked to pick her up and take her out for her favorite treat: ice cream. Sally loved spending the extra time with her Dad, but he always seemed distant. He would regularly check his watch or his phone, and often didn't listen to what hear her at all. Even though she loved having that one-on-one time, she wished her Dad would stop worrying about his work and pay more attention to her.*

Above, you can see that Sally's Dad was not being mindful. His frequent checking of his watch and his phone signified that he was somewhere else in his mind. Sometimes, he was so distant, he didn't even hear her talking! This can be damaging to relationships with other people and can lead to stress, discomfort, anger, and other unnecessary issues between two people. This is not a good state to be in, especially considering Sally is talking about her own Dad!

Situation 2: *Sally was spending time with her Dad, as they often did on Fridays after school. He liked to pick her up and take her out for her favorite treat: ice cream. Sally loved spending extra time with her Dad. He always gave her all of the attention she needed and wanted during this time. He would talk to her about how her day went, ask her how school was doing, and even offer to help her practice more for the cheerleading team! Sally knew he was a busy man because of his demanding job, so she really appreciated that he took the time to put his work aside and give her his full attention for their time together.*

Above, Sally's Dad was being mindful. He was actively involved in the moment, he was listening to his daughter and engaging in meaningful conversation with her. He put away his phone and stopped checking his watch, and he really gave his daughter the quality time that they both needed. This time would nurture their relationship together, and create a more powerful and meaningful bond between the father and daughter, which is valuable for both of them.

Being mindful has the ability to offer a significant number of emotional benefits. The more mindful you are, the more present you are in the moment. This makes your experiences much more valuable and can help bring you more joy, a greater sense of connection, reduced stress, and greater fulfillment in life.

Health Benefits

Believe it or not, mindfulness does have actual physical health benefits. The more mindful you are in life, the healthier you are going to be. While this phenomenal technique isn't so powerful that it can cure ailments, it does have the ability to prevent and reduce the occurrence of a number of symptoms and diseases. There's a very practical and logical reason as to why, too.

When you are mindful, you are present in the moment. This translates to a number of different benefits that contribute to the increased quality of health that can be drawn from being a mindful person. First, being more present in the moment means that you are less stressed and agitated. Remember all of the emotional benefits you learned about a moment ago? Someone who is in a less stressed and calmer state of mind is much less likely to experience common symptoms and diseases that are born from stress. These include but are not limited to: high blood pressure; headaches; tense muscles; a sore jaw; and even some cardiac ailments. Stress has the ability to cause a number of different diseases in our body. While becoming less stressed isn't the *only* way to prevent or eliminate these ailments and diseases, it is a great way to reduce your risk of getting them to begin with. It can also assist you in eliminating them when used alongside a qualified health plan set out by your health provider.

In addition to allowing you to eliminate or at least reduce symptoms and diseases, mindfulness can also allow you to be more in sync with your body. When this occurs, you will be much more likely to take care of your body in the way it needs to be taken care of.

For example, if you are thirsty, you will drink water. If you are hungry, you will eat. If you are mindful, you are likely going to choose a healthy and fulfilling food option over a sugary-filled quick-fix to your hunger. If you are sleepy, you will go to bed. So on, and so forth. The more mindful you are, the more in sync with your body you will be, and the more likely you will take care of it in a way that keeps it healthy and working optimally. Additionally, if you notice something wrong, you will be able to schedule an appointment with your doctor right away, as opposed to ignoring it for several weeks because you are unaware of it at first.

As you can see, mindfulness has a high number of health benefits, beyond emotional ones. When you are mindful, you reduce your risk of contracting ailments and diseases that can greatly decrease your quality of life, or in extreme cases, kill you. This practice is a wonderful technique to stay in tune with your body, listen to what it needs, and nourish it in ways that allow you to flourish and work in the most optimal way.

Worldly Benefits

If you thought mindfulness only had a benefit on yourself, you were wrong! Mindfulness is a practical and strategic way to benefit the world around you, as well! This amazing technique allows you the opportunity to improve your world through several different ways.

First, when you are mindful, you are much less likely to engage in arguments or conflict with other people. When you do choose to engage in a conflict, you will be much more rational about your approach, and the situation will likely diffuse quickly. If it doesn't, you will recognize that no benefit is being drawn from the experience, and you will remove yourself from the situation. Mindful people are generally much less emotionally charged in a negative format than those who are not mindful. They are more likely to be able to handle anger and stresses strategically, which means that even their "opponent" will end the situation in a more calm and rational way. This may simply diffuse one set of bad emotions, or it could trickle and encourage the other person to go learn about mindfulness and practice being more peaceful and calm in their own lives. You never know!

Additionally, the more we are in sync with the world around us, the more we are going to experience value from the world, and give value to the world. We are more likely to notice people who are struggling, so we can offer help. We are more likely to experience the highest joy we possibly can, which truly is contagious! Many other people who experience your intoxicating joy are going to turn around and experience some of their own as a result!

Finally, people who are mindful are generally a lot more considerate of the Earth itself. They tend to take better care of the world around them through many measures, including but not limited to: recycling, not littering, helping clean up after others, taking care of plants and animals, and more! Doing all of this contributes to the healthy production and growth of the planet, which means that you are assisting it in thriving and maintaining its health!

Being a mindful person adds greater value to life, for the person who is mindful both emotionally and mentally, for the people around them, and for the Earth itself. When people are mindful, they are less stressed and more at peace, they are more engaged with those around them, and they are much more likely to experience greater fulfillment out of their lives. This practice and technique is potentially one of the most valuable ones you could ever teach yourself.

Chapter 2: Creating the Calm

The very first step in becoming more mindful in your life is learning to create the calmness. Or, in other words, learning to relax your mind and let things be. In this chapter, you will learn exactly how you can let go of everything that is stressing you out from your past and your future, and focus strictly on the present moment. This is really the biggest lesson in mindfulness that you need to learn. Once you learn what mindfulness is and how it feels, you will have a much easier time applying it to various situations throughout your life.

Learning to be mindful is truly a process. You are going to start out and probably have a hard time with it at first, and then you are going to continue practicing it until you are a master at it. Once you learn how to become mindful the first time, practicing mindfulness constantly becomes easier every single time you practice it. So, if you ever find you've gone a few days particularly stressed out and lacking mindfulness, you will know exactly what you need to do in order to reclaim your peace through mindfulness.

The first thing is understanding exactly what mindfulness is. Essentially, mindfulness is a form of being present in the moment. It is a time where you prevent yourself from becoming absorbed in thoughts of the past or the perceived future, and you let yourself experience exactly what is materializing right in front of you, right in that moment. So, you are noticing the colors of your surroundings, the smells, the feelings, the tastes if there are any, and the sounds. You really want to enrich as many of your senses with each experience as you possibly can, *and* take the time to actually notice them.

The easiest way to become mindful in a moment is to practice the 5-4-3-2-1 technique. This technique became popular within the last few years for good reason. It is an excellent way to help reclaim your current moment and encourage your mind to focus on what is physically going on around you, rather than straying away into other parts of your mind. In order to practice this method, all you have to do is quietly tell yourself five things you can see, four things you can touch, three things you can hear, two things you can smell and one thing you can taste. This helps you focus on exactly what is happening in the present, and keeps your mind actively paying attention to your current experiences.

You should practice this technique any time you want to become mindful of the moment around you. Observing your experiences with all of your senses is a great way to fully immerse yourself in the present and truly gain all of the value it has to offer. The more you practice this, the easier it will become for you.

You may be wondering when you should use mindfulness. Of course, it's not practical to expect that you are going to be mindful every minute of every day. Even mindfulness masters can't do that, so no matter how long and hard you practice, you are going to experience moments where your mind strays away from you. That is completely normal and absolutely okay. The human brain is a natural wanderer and part of being mindful and experiencing life as fully as possible is recognizing that and giving your brain the permission to do so. The goal is not to have you constantly having to stop your brain from doing what it naturally wants to do. Instead, it's controlling your brain to not wander when the situation warrants for you to be present. When you are working, when you are waking up, when you are eating something new, when you are spending time with people you love, and many other situations are more fully experienced when you practice mindfulness while doing so. However, that's not to say that you can never allow your mind to wander. In this short list below, you will learn more techniques about mindfulness and when you should apply this strategy in your life.

Give Yourself Mind Permission to Wander

Since your mind naturally wants to wander, sometimes the best way to become mindful is to let your mind wander. This may sound counterproductive, but the reality is that it will actually save and enhance your mindfulness practice. When your mind wants to wander and you're consistently having to tell it no, you are not going to be practicing mindfulness because you will instead be having an internal conflict with your mind. Rather than allowing that to go on and then stressing yourself out further, you can simply give yourself permission to let your mind wander. You can let it go for a set period of time, say like five minutes, and then when that time is up, you can gently bring your mind back to the present moment and carry on with your mindfulness practice. This sounds like a paradox, but sometimes being mindful of your desire to let your mind wander is the best way to do it!

Practice Mindfulness During Regular Routines

Often times, our regular routines become mundane and repetitive. We do them so often that we no longer think about what we're doing, we just do it. You may notice this to be the case for many instances in your day and life, for example: brushing your teeth, driving to work, large portions of your work day, coming home from work, making supper, and more. These are all a great time to practice being mindful. When we tend to "check out" for these activities, we can stop feeling present in the moment and start working on autopilot. Not only does this detract from mindfulness, but it can actually lead to your emotional run-down, and sometimes even dangerous situations, such as if you are on mental autopilot while driving to work. These are some of the best times to practice being mindful. You may find that your routine is a lot more fun than you were experiencing, or that there are new and more efficient ways you could be doing things!

Switch It Up!

If you are feeling that your life is too full of routines, another great way to practice mindfulness and really gain a lot of value from it is to switch up your routines! If you always wake up, stretch, go to the bathroom, turn on the coffee pot and then flick on the morning news, then try something else for a change! Wake up, go to the bathroom, set the kettle to boil and make yourself a nice beverage and then drink it on the balcony! You may choose to take a different route to work, walk a different way to your office, sit down in a different way, or do any number of different things to help switch up the pace of things. When you break the routine, you give your mind a bit of a break from the autopilot mode and you encourage it to pay attention by making it interested in what is going on. Sometimes becoming mindful of your routine and during your routines will actually lead you to make changes because you will realize you have been doing unnecessary extras, or that certain things aren't as efficient or effective anymore. Being mindful and giving yourself permission to switch it up is a great way to get your brain active in your daily routines again and give it a break from the regular day-to-day activities that can become boring and mundane.

Practice Mindfulness as Soon as You Wake

When we wake up, many of us don't jump straight out of bed. Even if you do, it is still a great time to practice mindfulness. Since you have been asleep for a while, you have been on somewhat of a mental vacation from your body. During this time, your brain has been wandering for several hours, typically. So, this is a great time to practice mindfulness! See if you can notice the light shining in through the window, the sensation of the blankets or the air on your skin, the sound of the birds or of other people in your home, and any smells and tastes you may notice.

The morning is a great time to practice mindfulness because it allows you to start your day off with being more aware of your surroundings. They say that when we start our day out a certain way, it can make it easier to carry on that task throughout the rest of the day. With that logic, if you are mindfulness first thing in the morning, you will likely find it much easier to be mindful throughout the rest of your day. It is a great way to set the tone, have a positive morning, and really create the perfect setting to allow the rest of your day to be mindful and peaceful.

Short and Sweet Wins the Treat

Remember how you learned that mindfulness isn't something that you are expected to, or even capable of, practicing for every minute of the day? If you struggle with mindfulness, sometimes it's easiest just to be mindful in short bursts. In fact, science has proven that if you are mindful for short periods several times during the day as opposed to one single longer period, you will gain greater benefit from it. With that knowledge, it is a good idea to allow yourself to become present for a few minutes at a time throughout your entire day, instead of expecting yourself to become mindful about everything you do all of the time, or only practicing it once a day for lengthy time frames. Being mindful doesn't have to be a long and hard technique that you put a significant amount of effort into for several hours each day. Instead, draw your mind in when you remember to, and practice doing it more and more each day.

Practice Mindfulness When You're Waiting

When we are waiting for things, we tend to become stressed out, bored, or even agitated. Most humans do not like to wait, which means that this is a great time for you to practice mindfulness! Instead of letting your mind wander down the rabbit hole of negativity that leads you to feel uncomfortable and upset about a situation that you can't control, practice being calm and peaceful. Notice the other people in the lineup, recognize that you're all waiting together, listen to the sounds around you, see what else you can notice about the particular situation. You will be surprised at how enjoyable it can be to stop and observe those around us during these periods where we're forced to wait. You can even do this if you're waiting to be taken off of hold on the phone, when you're waiting for an appointment in a lobby, or at any other time that you find yourself waiting around. It is a great chance to regroup and reframe an otherwise bland, or even stressful activity!

Assign a Reminder Prompt to Help You

Many people find it extremely helpful to associate something with mindfulness and use it as an opportunity to remind themselves to be mindful. There are many ways you may do this in your life, and how you personally choose to do it will be unique to you. However, it can be extremely beneficial to have something that you associate with mindfulness that will prompt you to practice mindfulness throughout your day. Some people choose something simple such as a bracelet or a certain trinket they carry around in their pocket, so that any time they touch, see or notice the item, they are reminded to practice mindfulness. In this day and age, we are also granted with the gift of technology. If you find having a trinket around with you doesn't remind you to stay mindful, you may prefer to set reminders in your phone or switch your phone background to something that will prompt you to practice mindfulness throughout the day. However, you choose to do it, having these prompts are a great way to remember to practice mindfulness and infuse it into your everyday life. Again, you don't have to practice mindfulness constantly, but practicing it in short bursts several times throughout the day is an excellent way to increase the value you gain from mindfulness, emotionally, physically, and otherwise.

Practice Meditation

Meditation is essentially a prolonged practice of mindfulness. Many people love using meditation as a means to infuse an even higher quality of mindfulness into their daily routines. Meditation is an excellent opportunity to objectively explore the thoughts in your mind and guide yourself to a new state of calm. This is especially helpful if you feel that something has been bugging you for a while. Meditation may seem difficult, especially to a beginner, but it is actually quite simple. In order to practice meditation, all you need to do is give yourself a set amount of time, set a timer on your phone if you need to, and then close your eyes and release your control over your mind. Every time you notice your mind has wandered "too far", you can gently practice bringing it back to the center. Some choose to hold an image in their mind, and when their thoughts wander, at any time that they've noticed it's happened, they gently bring their mind back to the thought of the image. You may find that your mind wanders a lot, or that it can be hard to even realize that it has done so. This is completely natural, and you will experience this for the majority of your meditation practices, even when you become a master at it. The best thing you can do is give yourself the permission to practice meditation without judging yourself for how you do so.

The Conclusion

Mindfulness is an ongoing practice that you will learn about as you continue to practice the techniques you have been provided with here. You may realize that it is hard at first, but in time you will get much better at it. Remember, there are going to be times that you struggle with mindfulness, even when you are a master. The best way to keep yourself on the path of mindfulness is to set reminders and encourage yourself to practice mindfulness, especially during mundane and routine activities that we generally set ourselves to "autopilot" for us to complete. You will likely find that the more you practice, the easier it is to remember to do so. Like other skills, mindfulness is one you will master if you practice it often enough. This way, if you ever find that you have gone a prolonged period of time without mindfulness, it will be easy to draw it back into your life and pick up where you left off. This practice is not meant to be a stressful one or one that you worry about having to learn. Instead, it is one that will help you learn more about yourself and the world around you, while in turn providing you with significant benefits related to your health, your emotions, your mental wellbeing, and even the world around you.

Chapter 3: Peace in Pandemonium

There is one specific time when you may want to practice mindfulness, but you are having a difficult time. This is one of the hardest points to master mindfulness, and once you do so, you'll know that you are mindfulness master. The hardest time to practice and maintain mindfulness is when you are experiencing any form of conflict. Whether your conflict is internal with yourself, external with another human, or external with the environment you're in, conflict can create a great difficulty when it comes to practicing mindfulness. Consequently, it is one of the best times to practice mindfulness, as well.

The moment you notice you are in a situation that involves conflict, regardless of what type of conflict, you are going to want to use your learned practice to infuse mindfulness into the situation. This is going to quickly allow you to rationalize your emotions, adjust your action, and likely diffuse the situation quickly. You will enable yourself and that which you are in conflict with the gift of being respected and appreciated as it is, free of judgment. You allow yourself the permission to recognize the situation, honor your discomfort, and respond in such a way that allows all parties to be at peace with the resolution. Mindfulness during conflict is one of the most powerful ways to turn a difficult situation into something easier to manage. You are about to learn exactly how you can practice mindfulness during a difficult or conflicting situation, and how it is going to benefit your life in many ways beyond what simple daily mindfulness can do on its own.

The following acronym "RAIN" is a great skill to practice when you are experiencing conflict. This simple acronym will allow you to regain your mindfulness practice and use it as a means to eliminate the conflict you are currently experiencing. When you practice this, you will likely find that at first that it can be difficult. After you become used to using it, however, you will probably find that it becomes easier, or even second nature whenever you are being faced with conflict. The simplicity of this acronym makes it easy to remember, even during a hard situation, and can help you quickly diffuse the situation at hand.

Recognize the Conflict

The first and most important part of practicing mindfulness during conflict is recognizing that the conflict is occurring. You are likely not going to have the time or desire to practice the 5-4-3-2-1 strategy, as conflict is usually fast and heated. Instead, simply take the time to recognize the conflict. You should then give yourself a moment to become aware of your personal sensations. What are you feeling in your body and in your mind? What emotions are you bringing into this experience that may be making it harder for you to be rational? You may want to form judgments around these thoughts or feelings or try and ignore them because they are unpleasant, but the reality is that you need to recognize them, and the best way to do so is to eliminate judgment and simply just recognize as much as you can.

Once you recognize your thoughts and emotions, as well as physical experiences, it will be easier to give them a label. Often when we are in conflict, the only emotion we feel we are experiencing is anger. Generally, that is not the case. We are instead feeling a number of emotions, or one particularly strong emotion that is uncomfortable and often mislabeled as anger. It could be jealousy, hurt, sadness, worry, or any other number of emotions. Recognizing the exact emotions that you experience will give you the opportunity to address them appropriately. It also gives you an opportunity to have a greater awareness of yourself, and potentially learn some important things about yourself that you may not have learned about otherwise.

Allow Yourself (and Others) To Own Their Opinion

Once you have recognized the situation, your personal sensations and emotions, and the particular underlying emotion or emotions that you are experiencing, you need to practice "allowing". This means that you are just allowing life to be. You allow yourself to have your right to your opinion, and you allow others to do the same. You should allow yourself to have the experience of the negative emotions, even if it hurts, and allow yourself to learn from what the emotions are trying to teach you. A great way to give yourself permission to allow things to happen as they are is to mentally say "yes" to your emotions. Allow yourself to accept your emotions as they are, and allow them to be experienced fully. Doing this is going to give you the opportunity to quickly and completely address the emotions in the situation, rather than bottling them up and drawing them out later at an equally destructive time.

Investigate the Situation

Sometimes when you recognize the situation and allow the emotions to be felt and allow yourself to simply experience life, you will feel the conflict quickly fade. Other times, it may persist. If you are experiencing a type of conflict that is particularly persistent and you are having a hard time managing it, you may want to move on to the step called "investigate". This gives you the ability to further explore the situation and grow from it. The following questions are a great way to help yourself address emotions, especially if you are not sure exactly what you are feeling, as well as address the situation, especially if you are not sure of exactly what has happened:

1. "What is the tone of the experience?" (Negative, neutral, or positive)
2. "What specific event triggered this conflict?"
3. "What about this event made it triggering to me?"
4. "Have there been similar events in the past that triggered me before?"
5. "What is the story that I am telling myself about these particular feelings?"
6. "What is the story that these particular feelings are trying to tell me?"
7. "Are there any alternative stories that exist for these feelings I am experiencing?"

8. "Is the story I am telling myself actually realistic?"
9. "Do I have any bodily sensations connected to this particular experience?"

The more you investigate, the more you are going to learn from the situation. You will often find surprising and interesting answers that help draw you deeper into your own existence and understand why certain things make you feel certain ways, especially if they seem to be a trend. This will allow you to become more mindful of the conflict itself, but will also allow you to become more mindful of you as a person and how you can nurture yourself in a way that will reduce or eliminate these conflicts going forward.

If you are having a hard time discovering the emotional attachments to the conflict, or are unsure as to why they are affecting you, it can be a good idea to address these with a series of investigation questions. This will allow you to gain greater clarity on the situation and respond in a better way in the future.

Non-Identification from the Situation

While this step is not a step that you take action on, it is one that is involved in the conflict-resolution process when using mindfulness. You will know you have successfully used mindfulness in your conflicting situation when you are no longer identifying with the situation. Instead of saying things like "why me?" or "what did I do to deserve this?", you will be in a position where you understand the conflict and recognize it was simply a difficult situation. Your perspective will be shifted, and you will notice that you no longer identify with the situation and that you instead recognize it for what it is, allow it to be, and carry on.

Mindfulness can be particularly hard when you are in a conflicting situation. It can be easy to become immersed in the feelings you are experiencing and feed into them, whether they are ones of sadness, anger, hurt, or other difficult emotions. When we feel these, we tend to ignore *why* and focus more on eliminating them through action. That is why we often associate yelling, screaming, temper tantrums, and other negative elimination actions with these emotions. The more we get stuck in our heads and fail to address the situation in a mindful manner, the deeper it seeds into our bodies and makes it harder for us to respond in any other way. That is why it is crucial that you practice mindfulness, especially during conflicting situations.

Added Health Benefits of Mindfulness During Conflict

As mentioned previously, there are added benefits of practicing mindfulness during conflicting situations. These benefits are largely related to mental health and have a lasting value in our lives. The first way mindfulness during conflict benefits you is that it essentially trains your brain to react in a more peaceful and rational way with certain triggers. This allows your brain to learn new patterns that will make it easier for you to act with mindfulness in future conflicting situations. The more you practice mindfulness during conflict, the easier it will become!

The second way that mindfulness helps during conflict is by allowing you to address your internal experiences related to specific triggers. This gives you the ability to look deeper within' yourself and truly understand why things are difficult for you. The more you practice understanding your conflicts on this deeper level, the more you are going to understand yourself and the greater your mindfulness practice will be. It will also give you the ability to work through residual triggers and make it easier for you to eliminate those triggers altogether, so you won't have to worry about them coming up for you anymore!

You are halfway done!

Congratulations on making it to the halfway point of the journey. Many try and give up long before even getting to this point, so you are to be congratulated on this. You have shown that you are serious about getting better every day. I am also serious about improving my life, and helping others get better along the way. To do this I need your feedback. Click on the link below and take a moment to let me know how this book has helped you. If you feel there is something missing or something you would like to see differently, I would love to know about it. I want to ensure that as you and I improve, this book continues to improve as well. Thank you for taking the time to ensure that we are all getting the most from each other.

Chapter 4: The Practical Practice

Despite what you have already learned, there are many more ways still to practice mindfulness in your life. The more practical the application is, the easier it will be to practice and the more you are going to learn from it. For some people, setting aside time to practice mindfulness every day is simply not something they are willing to do. While it can be beneficial to do so, there are other even more practical ways to infuse mindfulness into your day, should you decide you prefer to do it that way.

In this chapter, we are going to further explore the practicality of mindfulness, and how you can use it in your day to day life. These simple moments in your life are a great time to practice mindfulness and really draw the best value from it that you possibly can. When you are practicing mindfulness, you may wish to start with a very practical application, then gradually increase the amount of time you spend practicing this habit. Whichever way you choose to do it, it is completely up to you!

Be Mindful When You Eat

Many of us are in such a rush that when we eat, we plow through our meals as quickly as we can. The experience of food has been largely lost on us, especially in modern times where fast-paced life and fast-paced food are the norm. One of the best times you can introduce mindfulness into your day is while you are eating. Being mindful when you eat is an incredible way to turn eating into a pleasurable experience. You will learn what exactly you like and what you don't like, you will give yourself the chance to thoroughly taste the foods you are eating, and you will allow yourself the opportunity to truly enjoy the experience of eating. As well, when you are full, you will recognize that and stop eating, which means you will always feel satisfied and fulfilled after a meal, instead of overfull or uncomfortable. Many people who choose to eat mindfully find that they stay away from foods that are distasteful and unhealthy, like fast foods, and start to enjoy more quality foods, as well.

You don't have to reserve mindfulness for the process of eating, alone, either. You can also practice mindfulness when you are cooking. Take time to observe all of the colors and scents coming together, notice the way the food looks as it becomes closer and closer to being completed. The more you invest in being mindful during your eating experience, the more enjoyable eating is going to be. A great reason to practice mindfulness during your meals is that in doing so, you will spend more time paying attention to your body. That way, when you are full, you will finish. You may notice you become full much sooner than you'd previously thought. This is a great way to stay healthy and allow your body the opportunity to take a break once it's done. Many people who eat mindfully find that they no longer gorge themselves on meals and that they enjoy themselves a lot more. Cooking and eating are a great opportunity to practice mindfulness and truly experience the joy and satisfaction that food has to offer when it is appreciated appropriately.

When You're Dwelling On the Past

Virtually everyone spends time thinking about the past, and at one time or another, we've all caught ourselves dwelling on it. The past is something that can be a valuable learning tool, but it can also detract from our present and future if we start to dwell on it. Many people stop using the past as a learning experience and start using it as a punishment to keep themselves from repeating things they did in the past that caused pain in their lives. What this does is harm them every single time they decide to invest more of their valuable time and emotion into this thought. The best thing you can do when this is happening is become mindful.

Being mindful about your past, particularly when you are dwelling on it, means that you will spend time recognizing that it is in the past. Instead of using it as a weapon against yourself or a punishment, you will start to use it as an opportunity to learn and grow. You will recognize why it hurt you, and what has made you cling on to that experience for so long. You will also have the opportunity to learn how you get through difficult times, and how they can assist you with growth. It won't necessarily make it easier to overcome future internal conflicts, but it will definitely give you a blueprint to effectively get there.

While Driving

Many people these days spend a great deal of time in our cars. Unfortunately, a lot of people also become so used to driving that they are no longer mindful of the experience itself. This is why many accidents happen: people become what we like to call "over confident" and they get into an accident. In other words, they became so used to driving that they stopped paying as much attention and respecting the danger that coincides with driving. A great way to change this up is to practice mindfulness while you are driving. When you are driving, you can practice mindfulness by spending more time noticing what is around you, paying attention to your mirrors, and watching your speed. You can take a few deep breaths when you're at stoplights and regroup yourself. Sometimes, a great way to enhance your mindfulness when driving is to turn off the music and really pay attention to the moment around you. This change in the familiar sound that fills your car can really help trigger you to become more mindful. Using time spent driving in your car is a great opportunity to practice mindfulness, as well as eliminate the "overconfidence" factor that can be a major risk when people are too comfortable with their driving patterns and routines.

When You Arrive at Work

So many people arrive at work and immediately become stressed out. In fact, they become stressed out on their way to work. This stress is often not provoked by anything aside from simply arriving at work. For many people, the workplace is an emotional trigger to experience stress or some other uncomfortable emotion. A great opportunity for practicing mindfulness is when you first arrive at work. Take time to notice how you are feeling, and what sort of physical sensations are attached to those feelings. Then, you can also take the time to consider why those feelings occur, and how they are truly affecting your day-to-day life. The reality is, many of us, if not all of us, have to work and keep our jobs. Since that is a factor we cannot change, it is not valuable to allow it to cause us significant stress and internal turmoil each day. Instead, you can address these emotions and practice mindfulness to allow yourself to realistically perceive the experience and draw more enjoyment out of your working experiences.

On Your Work Break

Another great time to ground yourself is when you're taking a break at work. This mindfulness experience allows you to regroup from any stress that your work may have caused up until that point, and then start working again with a new, more peaceful frame of mind. Being mindful at work is very important because this is where many of us tend to draw stress from. The more you are able to become mindful of your experiences, shift your focus and perspective, and learn to enjoy your working experience, the less stressful the workplace is going to become for you. A great way to do this is on your breaks.

Alternatively, if you are having a particularly stressful day, it can be beneficial to take a short unscheduled break to practice mindfulness. You can do this in a simple two-minute trip to the washroom. All you need to do is head into the bathroom, and start practicing your mindfulness. You can use the 5-4-3-2-1 method to ground yourself and keep yourself in the present moment. In the process, it will let you take a second to regroup and shift your focus to something more positive that is associated with your work. This is a great way to relieve sudden and urgent stressors that can arise while we are at work.

It is a really good idea to spend a few minutes out of your work day focusing on mindfulness. This is the perfect opportunity to quickly relieve ourselves from stressful emotions and thoughts and allow ourselves to become present in the moment and remember the bigger picture. Doing this will make your workplace less stressful, and help make arriving at work a more enjoyable experience for you.

Grounding Yourself with Noise

We all hear a lot of noise during the day: phones ringing, doorbells chiming, the sounds of cars going by, and so many other sounds. These are all a great opportunity to practice mindfulness. When you are busy with something, you may notice that these sounds all sort of drop to the background and are no longer something you recognize. You should take the opportunity to recognize these sounds whenever you can, and allow yourself to use them as a prompt to quickly ground yourself. Bring yourself back into the present moment, recognize what is going on around you, and become mindful of your current situation. Most often, this is a great way to alleviate stress and become more present each day. You can use this when you are working, when you are at home, or at any other time during your day when you are preoccupied with your thoughts and want to become more focused on the present moment and the world around you.

Leaving Work

Due to many people working jobs, the workplace truly becomes a great opportunity for practicing mindfulness. Perhaps one of the things that makes this the best place is because it is also the place that most people associate with high-stress levels. This may be because the workplace is a place where we all feel pressure to attend in order to maintain our lifestyles, but many of us are not passionate about our jobs. It can lead to a very mundane, boring, and unhappy experience for many people who are going to work. Even if you don't totally dislike your job or have any particular experiences there that cause you to be able to pinpoint your stress to any one thing, it can still become an unhappy place if you are not inspired by it and passionate about the work you are doing.

Practicing mindfulness is a great way to change that. Since you are already practicing when you arrive and when you are on breaks, it makes sense that another great time to practice mindfulness is when you leave work. Doing this gives you the amazing opportunity of leaving behind the days' stressors and appreciating the current moment. At the moment you leave, you no longer have to worry about work duties until you come back. With that knowledge, you should spend time each day practicing mindfulness and leaving your work stressors behind so you can arrive home with a fresh state of mind. Doing this will make your home time much less stressful and more rejuvenating, making it easier to arrive at work the next time you are scheduled to do so.

Arriving Home from A Day Out

Another excellent time to practice mindfulness is when you arrive back home after being away for some time. You may be away due to work, shopping, a trip away, or any other number of things. Regardless of the reason, this is a great opportunity to practice mindfulness. Take a moment to notice the comfort of your home, the familiar surroundings around you, the people or animals that are there to greet you, and anything else that makes you feel comfortable. Do whatever you can to become even more immersed in the current moment. You may choose to diffuse essential oils, brew yourself a luxurious beverage, turn on some of your favorite music, or do any other number of things that will make the experience more peaceful and comforting. These activities will also help draw your awareness to the present situation, making it even more enjoyable for you.

The more you associate your home with peace, comfort, and calmness, the easier it will be to remain mindful when you are home. This is important because you want your home to be a space that is comfortable and safe for you. You should not feel like you have to compensate for difficult emotions or situations when you are in your home. Instead, it should feel like a sanctuary that allows you the opportunity to relieve yourself of the stressors of the external world, and truly enjoy your present moment.

There are many times that you can practice being mindfulness in practical applications. For some people, these opportunities for practicing mindfulness are the best ones, because they allow you to be the most present without having to go out of your way to do so. You do not have to use prompts or "sit on the sidelines" for any given period of time to be mindful. Instead, you simply allow yourself the chance to become mindful at routine moments and turn it into an enjoyable practice that you look forward to on a daily basis. It should be a chance to regroup and recover from anything that may be drawing your attention out and causing stress in your daily life.

Chapter 5: Maintaining Mindfulness

Mindfulness is something that we must practice, constantly. It is not something we achieve ones and maintain forever. Rather, it is something that we must practice on a daily basis in order to maintain. Knowing this, you may find it sometimes is harder to maintain your state of mindfulness than it is for other times. Allow this to bring you peace, knowing that falling out of tune is completely normal. Additionally, the more you fall out of tune and regain your mindfulness, the easier it will be to regain it in the future.

Sometimes, it may be days or even weeks before you notice that you have fallen out of the routine of mindfulness. When you are brand new to the practice, it is easy to forget that you are working to be more mindful in your life. It is not uncommon for people to be extremely mindful for the first several days, and then just completely forget about it. Or, they may even become worn out. Sometimes, being mindful really forces us to confront emotional triggers that we are not interested in confronting. This can make it feel difficult to maintain and may make you feel like it is more comfortable to be ignorant than it is to be mindful. Realize that it is completely normal to run into these blocks, even for the most mindful people you will ever meet.

There are many ways you can contribute to maintaining your mindfulness, several of which we have already explored and discussed in this book. However, it is important to realize that it won't always be easy to maintain your mindfulness. As you've already learned, when there is chaos or confrontation, or when you are experiencing pandemonium, it can be difficult to maintain your mindfulness.

However, sometimes it's just difficult in general. When you are not already wired to a mindful state, it can be hard to remember to stay mindful. Sometimes, you might struggle to remember to do it, not just during hard times, but at any time, because you are not used to it. You may find that you don't realize you haven't been mindful until after the situation has already passed, and then feel guilty or regretful that you didn't do it differently.

There are several things you should realize and do if this occurs, which will help you maintain a mindful state, even if it's sometimes difficult to remember. Below, we are going to explore the various stages of regaining mindfulness, even when you are forgetful or hardwired to respond to situations in a different way.

Give Yourself Permission to Go Slow

Changes don't happen overnight, especially when you are talking about changes for things that you have been doing for many years, perhaps even your whole life. There are no magic formulas, genies or spells that you can use to help you instantaneously become a more mindful person. Instead, you will have to work towards being mindful every day of your life, even once you've already mastered the art of mindfulness.

It is important that you give yourself permission to go as slow as you need to. You are not going to be able to respond to every single situation with mindfulness just because you've decided that's what you want to do. Instead, you are going to find that you will actually rarely respond with mindfulness at first, and that may be very frustrating for you. Realize that you will need to take your time and respect your need to go slow and take this as a learning process. The changes that last the longest are the ones that can take the longest to create. The more effort you have to put in to get yourself into a changed state of mind, the more likely that state will last you. Even if you have to maintain it.

It may take you several weeks, maybe even months to become mindful. Some people even take years to master it. You never know how long it will take you, because of all of the different elements that go into being mindful. Your unique blocks and resistances, lifestyle, and existing level of mindfulness, plus many other things will all contribute to how quickly you can become mindful the majority of the time.

Start Recognizing Triggers

The very first step to switching over to *mindfulness* as your new full-time lifestyle is recognizing triggers. If you are having a hard time maintaining your mindfulness practice because of forgetfulness or a later realization that you "could have" responded with mindfulness, it may be because you are not recognizing your triggers. Take some time and start realizing what your triggers are. These will change on a regular basis, just like life does, so you will need to consistently maintain a check-in process where you recognize what your triggers are and learn why they cause you to respond in certain ways. The more you understand this, the easier it will be for you to maintain mindfulness.

It is not beneficial to judge your triggers. Doing this can cause you to create new blocks and resistances which may further drive you away from a mindful state. Instead, you simply want to recognize what they are. This is an opportunity for you to look deeper within yourself and work on it. At first, there is nothing more that you need to do other than to simply recognize these triggers. Remember, changes don't happen overnight. Instead, you are going to need to take your time. Once you recognize these triggers, practice recognizing them in action. Every time a trigger of yours occurs, recognize it has happened and allow yourself to experience it. Don't encourage any changes yet, just recognize these triggers in action. You will need to practice recognizing new triggers every time one occurs in your life, which is why it is such an important step in maintaining your mindfulness practice.

Create Your Ideal Response

Once you recognize your new triggers and are very confident in your ability to become mindful about them as they are actively happening, you are ready to create your ideal response. You may have already been thinking of an ideal response up until now, but now is the time to think of a practical, mindful and realistic response that you could use when these triggers arise. This should represent your ideal method of how you would want to respond to a trigger.

For example, let's imagine that a particular person makes you angry when you are speaking to them. It gets to the point that you no longer have to hear anything from them at all for you to become angry. Rather, you just become angry from seeing them in general! In this instance, it may seem like the person is the trigger. However, it is likely something that this person has done, said or expressed in the past that has created the trigger. This, in turn, led to a situation where every time you see this person, you think about that experience.

Your ideal response may be that every time you see this person, you feel no emotions at all. You don't necessarily need to feel good or better when you see them. You just need to eliminate the uncomfortable and charged emotions, like anger and hurt. Knowing this, you may set the intention that every time you see this person, you will no longer feel emotionally charged. Instead, you will just feel neutral.

The above situation and correlating ideal response system can be applied to virtually any trigger you experience in life. Once you recognize the trigger and understand when it is actively happening, you'll likely start gaining more information about *why* it happens when you are in that specific situation. Knowing that, you can create an ideal response on how you would rather feel and respond to the situation, versus how you are actively responding. Make sure that the ideal response is something realistic and achievable. Setting the bar too high may prevent you from achieving it at all.

Use Your Ideal Response at Least 25% Of The Time

Again, you need to be prepared to move slowly. You cannot expect that just because you have recognized the trigger and set the intention that you will now respond perfectly every single time. That in itself just isn't realistic. Instead, you should be prepared to respond your ideal way at least 25% of the time. This allows you the opportunity to prepare to respond that way, but also gives you immediate permission that if the situation doesn't go as you desire for it to go, it won't be a "failure" on your part. Rather, it is just one of the 75% of instances where mindfulness hasn't taken root yet!

When you notice the trigger, think about your ideal response. The first several times, you may only think about the response and how you may have made it work in that situation. Eventually, you will arrive at a situation where the ideal response feels like it naturally wants to take place from you. This is the time where you can start practicing it. The more you practice it, the easier it will become for you.

It is important to understand that this is a major part of maintaining mindfulness. Sometimes, you may put in all of the effort to eliminate a trigger, only for it to come back again. If you notice a trigger has fully come back to you, you will need to revert back to this step and practice integrating your ideal response. You may even need to adjust your ideal response to be something more appropriate and fitting so that it is easier for you to respond to it.

Realize that this part of the process takes a long time. It may even take you a long time just to get to the 25% mark. Again, give yourself the chance to take as much time as you need, and don't hold judgment for yourself or the situation when you need time. Giving yourself this permission is the best way to make sure that you don't feel as though you are failing, and that you allow yourself to respond in the most comfortable way. Believe it or not, the more you take the pressure off of yourself to act a certain way, the easier it will be for you to act the way you actually want to act. Eventually, it will come extremely naturally.

Practice the 80/20 Rule

Moving to the 80/20 rule is sometimes gradual, but you should keep this rule in mind as your destination point. While it will be difficult to get here right away, eventually this is where you should aim to end up. It is natural that we may experience triggers, even long after we have worked through them and moved on. Sometimes, it's just something that happens. If you can stay mindful at least 80 percent of the time, then you are doing well. More, and you are golden!

Having a rule like the 80/20 rule gives you permission to make mistakes, without having to consider that as a complete failure of your mindfulness practice. It can take off a great deal of stress and pressure, and make it even easier to be mindful the majority of the time. This works even better because it makes you mindful about your mindfulness. That way, on the times you make a mistake, rather than beating yourself up you can take a look at *why* the trigger happened again, and address it. This will give you the best chance of making sure that you can eliminate triggers once and for all.

Watch Deep Rooted Changes Take Place

The longer you practice mindfulness, the deeper it will root itself in your life. Eventually, you will always address things in this method: by recognizing a trigger, addressing it, creating an alternative response, and enforcing that response at least most of the time. Over time, this will be a natural method for you to address virtually everything in your life, and that will ultimately shift you from a life of ignorance towards your troubles and into a life of mindfulness.

Mindfulness is not an overnight practice that can be mastered right away. Instead, you will have to practice and maintain your practice for the rest of your life. It will become much easier in time, but even when you are a master at mindfulness, you may still find there will be times where you struggle to be mindful. This is because life is ever-changing and we are emotionally charged beings that will sometimes react instead of respond.

However, you will notice in time that many deep-rooted and powerful changes take place in your life that will guide you in the direction of mindfulness. As this practice becomes more natural to you, you will realize that you are mindful at least 80% of the time in your entire life. You may not notice the changes as they are occurring, but one day you will look back and see just how far you have come!

Always Journal About It

If you are not one to recognize changes that happen in your own life, a good way to start recognizing them is to journal about it. The more you journal about your experiences, the more you can analyze them and make changes, as well as see how far you have come. Journaling has many great purposes when it comes to maintaining your mindfulness practice.

First off, when you journal you can truly gain a greater insight as to how far you have come. You will start to see exactly where you were when you started, and where you are now. You will likely notice that your ability to make changes become quicker and quicker the longer that you practice your mindfulness strategies, and also that you are more capable of adapting to harder situations.

Additionally, journaling is a great way to identify triggers, understand your blocks, and really gain a deeper insight as to what you are going through. Then, you can make more mindful and realistic approaches to how you will handle the situation and what you will do about it. Sometimes, writing about it can significantly help you alleviate a good portion of the stress that is associated with any given situation. As well, you may notice certain trends that occur in regards to your triggers or emotions and have a greater idea as to how you can increase the peace and positivity in your life through your mindfulness practices.

Journaling is an important part of making major life changes. It allows you to reflect deeper on what you are going through, track your progress, and empty yourself of many thoughts that may be using up extra space in your mind. Then, you can focus on the positive and powerful things you want to focus on, and you don't have to keep them in your mind taking up valuable real estate.

Respect, Love, and Honor Yourself Anyway

Some people who are practicing mindfulness may find it difficult to keep themselves positive and love themselves through the struggles. This is especially true when triggers are particularly emotional, or for those who are really early into their mindfulness practice. It can be easy to feel like you are failing, doing something wrong, or otherwise not having success in your practice. You may also find it easy to punish yourself or drag yourself down for what you are going through. It is important to realize that this is not beneficial and that it can actually detract from your mindfulness practice.

A major part of being mindful is feeling positive about yourself and your life. While this may not come easily to you, it is something you should focus on working towards. If you struggle with mindfulness for these reasons, one of your first missions should be to identify your triggers that get you feeling down on yourself and work through those first. You need to learn to practice respecting, loving and honoring yourself anyway.

There is nothing more detrimental to your mindfulness practice than being out of love and harmony with yourself. This can cause you to sabotage your ability to be mindful because you will tear yourself down every time you make a mistake. That is why it is crucial to give yourself room to make mistakes and to love yourself anyway. The easier you are on yourself and the less you hold yourself in contempt for your mistakes, the easier it will be for you to practice mindfulness in your life. It is very important that you give yourself space and permission to make mistakes, and that you love yourself anyway. This will allow you to be the most successful you can possibly be in your mindfulness practice.

As you can see, it won't always be easy to be mindful. Especially when you are brand new to the practice. Sometimes, it won't necessarily be chaos or difficult times that make it hard for you to be mindful. Sometimes, you will simply have a hard time remembering to practice this new way of life due to you being used to living life in a different way for so long. The best thing you can do is give yourself time and space, and draw yourself back to your practice whenever you realize you've strayed away. It may take a while to get there, but the more you practice, the more naturally it will come to you and the more successful you will be in your mindfulness.

Conclusion

Mindfulness is a powerful practice that has the ability to change your life in incredible ways. When you are mindful, you may experience better health, better emotional balances, and lower stress levels. You will give yourself the opportunity to relieve yourself from symptoms of stress. You also gain the ability to recognize what causes you discomfort, and practice working through it so that you can avoid experiencing those unpleasant experiences in the future. Of course, conflict cannot be eliminated, but you allow yourself to grow as a person and work through these conflicts more easily.

The practice of mindfulness can be done anywhere: in your car, at work, at home, or even when you're standing in line at the grocery store. You do not have to limit your practice to any one place or experience. As well, you do not need several minutes or hours to devote to a practice of mindfulness. Instead, you can practice it in as little as two minutes, if that is all you have to dedicate. In fact, it is better to practice mindfulness for a short period of times several times over the course of the day than it is to practice one long burst and never do it again for the rest of the day.

I hope that you learned how to use mindfulness in your daily habits and that it will greatly help you in achieving a more peaceful and empowered life. The practical methods in this book were shared in order to teach you how mindfulness works and exactly how you can work it into your busy routine.

If you enjoyed this book, I ask that you please take the time to rate it on Amazon Kindle. Your honest review would be greatly appreciated.

Thank you, and enjoy your mindful life!

Help me improve this book

While I have never met you, if you made it through this book I know that you are the kind of person that is wanting to get better and is willing to take on tough feedback to get to that point. You and I are cut from the same cloth in that respect. I am always looking to get better and I wish to not just improve myself, but also this book. If you have positive feedback, please take the time to leave a review. It will help other find this book and it can help change a life in the same way that it changed yours. If you have constructive feedback, please also leave a review. It will help me better understand what you, the reader, need to make significant improvements in your life. I will take your feedback and use it to improve this book so that it can become more powerful and beneficial to all those who encounter it.

REMEMBER TO JOIN THE GROUP NOW!

If you have not joined the Mastermind Self Development group yet, now is your time! You will receive videos and articles from top authorities in self development as well as a special group only offers on new books and training programs. There will also be a monthly member only draw that gives you a chance to win any book from your Kindle wish list!

If you sign up through this link
http://www.mastermindselfdevelopment.com/specialreport you will also get a special free report on the Wheel of Life. This report will give you a visual look at your current life and then take you through a series of exercises that will help you plan what your perfect life looks like. The workbook does not end there; we then take you through a process to help you plan how to achieve that perfect life. The process is very powerful and has the potential to change your life forever. Join the group now and start to change your life!
http://www.mastermindselfdevelopment.com/specialreport

You will also love these other great titles from Mastermind Self Development!

You will want to check out these other great titles Mastermind Self Development. All available in the Kindle store or you can just click on covers below.

getBook.at/learnfrench

myBook.to/learnspanish

You can also find these titles by searching them in the Kindle store on Amazon.

Positive Thinking

30 Days Of Motivation And Affirmations: Change Your "Mindset" & Fill Your Life With Happiness, Success, & Optimism!

By: Robert Norman

© Copyright 2016 - All rights reserved.

In no way is it legal to reproduce, duplicate, or transmit any part of this document by either electronic means or in printed format. Recording of this publication is strictly prohibited and any storage of this document is not allowed unless with written permission from the publisher. All rights reserved.

The information provided herein is stated to be truthful and consistent, in that any liability, in terms of inattention or otherwise, by any usage or abuse of any policies, processes, or directions contained within is the solitary and utter responsibility of the recipient reader. Under no circumstances will any legal responsibility or blame be held against the publisher for any reparation, damages, or monetary loss due to the information herein, either directly or indirectly.

Respective authors own all copyrights not held by the publisher.

Legal Notice:

This book is copyright protected. This is only for personal use. You cannot amend, distribute, sell, use, quote or paraphrase any part or the content within this book without the consent of the author or copyright owner. Legal action will be pursued if this is breached.

Disclaimer Notice:

Please note the information contained within this document is for educational and entertainment purposes only. Every attempt has been made to provide accurate, up to date and reliable complete information. No warranties of any kind are expressed or implied. Readers acknowledge that the author is not engaging in the rendering of legal, financial, medical or professional advice.

By reading this document, the reader agrees that under no circumstances are we responsible for any losses, direct or indirect, which are incurred as a result of the use of information contained within this document, including, but not limited to, —errors, omissions, or inaccuracies.

Free membership into the Mastermind Self Development Group!

For a limited time, you can join the Mastermind Self Development Group for free! You will receive videos and articles from top authorities in self development as well as a special group only offers on new books and training programs. There will also be a monthly member only draw that gives you a chance to win any book from your Kindle wish list!

If you sign up through this link http://www.mastermindselfdevelopment.com/specialreport you will also get a special free report on the Wheel of Life. This report will give you a visual look at your current life and then take you through a series of exercises that will help you plan what your perfect life looks like. The workbook does not end there; we then take you through a process to help you plan how to achieve that perfect life. The process is very powerful and has the potential to change your life forever. Join the group now and start to change your life!
http://www.mastermindselfdevelopment.com/specialreport

Table of Contents

© Copyright 2016 - All rights reserved.

Legal Notice:

Disclaimer Notice:

Table of Contents

What Power Does A Quote Have?

What Is An Affirmation?

How Are Daily Affirmations Going To Help?

Chapter 1: Affirmations – Why They Work and How to Use Them Effectively

Chapter 2: Phase One – Days One Through Eight

Chapter 3: Phase Three – Days Fifteen Through Twenty-Two

Chapter 4: Phase Four – Days Twenty-Three Through Thirty

Chapter 5: What if it Doesn't Work?

Chapter 6: Positive Affirmations for Success

Chapter 7: Positive Affirmations for Good Health

Chapter 8: Positive Affirmations for your Career

Chapter 9: Positive Affirmations for Motivation

Chapter 10: Preparing and Using Your Own Affirmations

Summary

Thank you for purchasing my book "Positive Thinking: 30 Days Of Motivation and Affirmations: Change Your "Mindset" & Fill Your Life With Happiness, Success, & Optimism." Choosing this book is the first step to bringing positive thinking into your life, the next step is to follow the day by day instructions as they are listed in the book and watch your life transform before your eyes.

One of the most efficient ways you can improve your life is by simply thinking in a more positive way. This isn't anything new, and probably isn't something that you haven't heard before as it is one of the most common pieces of advice that is given. However, it isn't as easy as it sounds. In fact, it is one of the most difficult things you are going to do. If it were as easy as it sounds, we would be living in a world full of people who see the glass as being half full and people wouldn't struggle with mental health.

You are probably wondering, if being more positive is the most effective way to bring more happiness into our lives, why aren't more of us more positive? There are a few reasons why it is incredibly difficult to become more positive.

How We Think It Is, Is How It Is – It's easy to confuse what has happened in our past as what is going to happen in the future. What we fail to realize is that what happened in our past does not have to equal the future. If you believe that it does, then it does. But, if you believe it doesn't, then it doesn't. It's that simple.

Changing Our Mind Set Is Hard – to become more positive, it is going to require that you change the way you are currently thinking. Changing how you view things isn't easy. Throughout our lives, we are told that things are the way they are. At no point are we told that we have the power to change it. Today I am telling you; you have the authority to change your mindset and become more positive.

Lack Of Energy And Motivation – Changing the way we think isn't easy. It takes a lot of emotional energy. If you are stressed out by work and your personal life and aren't eating or sleeping well you aren't going to have the energy that is required to change how you think. This is especially true if you aren't sure how being more positive is going to benefit you on a personal level.

So how do you get that motivation? How do you learn what the benefits to becoming more positive are? That is where this book comes in. This book is going to provide you with thirty days of affirmations and quotes that are designed to bring more positivity into your life.

This book is going to have each day on its own page, so you aren't distracted by the next day's reading. The thirty days are separated into four "phases" and each phase is going to include a challenge for you to complete throughout that phase. None of these challenges are going to be very difficult, and they were all designed with the purpose of making you more mindful of your thoughts and how they affect you and your life. Each day is going to include a quote as well as an affirmation for you to say to yourself.

What Power Does A Quote Have?

You are probably wondering if reading a quote is going to be enough to change how you are thinking and turn you into a more positive person. The answer is a resounding yes. Quotes have the power to coach us when we can relate to the situation the quote is discussing. They are often inspirational and give us the faith we need to know we are capable of accomplishing something. With each quote that you are going to read in this book, you are going to take the time to think about how it relates to a situation in your life. There is always some truth found in a quote though it may not directly be your truth, it certainly can pertain to a circumstance someone you may know might be going through. Remember, sharing hope and encouragement can return to you and yield a wonderful outcome.

Quotes often subconsciously subject imagery. As you read a quote you often envision yourself in that statement. You can immediately see yourself as the reason that quote is being said. Since quotes are an excerpt from another source it has often led others to desire to read more from that author in the search for more understanding.

There are countless philosophers, writers, poets, spiritual, and religious sources to draw wonderful and meaningful quotes from. There is a quote for everyone and it fits every kind of situation. Quotes can be seen as an art piece able to be dissected in any way that the viewer sees, and that is what makes them so direct and personal.

What Is An Affirmation?

Being able to have a thought, an aspiration, a dream is something that every human being who has ever lived has had and is undoubtedly something that we all are entitled to. Having the ability to have a goal in your mind and say "I can really do this" is the seed of self-motivation. There are also times when you may have self-doubt and are questioning your own position in your aspirations. This is the time when you must persevere and confirm all of what you want. You can achieve this through allowing yourself to give affirmation into your life. An affirmation is something you are going to say to yourself to undo the negative self-talk that you are currently experiencing. You might think you aren't experiencing any negative self-talk, but chances are that on some level, you probably are. Negative self-talk covers everything from believing you aren't going to be able to accomplish something to not liking something about yourself.

You are going to say your affirmations to yourself at least twice a day for five minutes at a time. This means that you are going to repeat your affirmation repeatedly for that five minutes. Say your affirmation slowly and allow the words to sink into your mind and become a part of your everyday thinking. Keep in mind that your environment that you speak your affirmation in is very important. You want to be in a place that is peaceful or meaningful to you. You may have young children who are going to and coming in from school, you may have a million things to do while getting ready for work in the morning. These may not be the right times for your daily affirmations to be spoken.

By reading these quotes and affirmations daily, you are reminding yourself every day of all of the good in your life. Quotes and affirmations have the power to change our thinking and help us to see something in ourselves that we want to change or overcome.

How Are Daily Affirmations Going To Help?

There are some great benefits to getting daily inspiration as well as saying daily affirmations.

- You are going to be aware of your daily thoughts and words, which is going to reduce the amount of negative thoughts that are going to be able to enter your mind.

- The daily practice is going to help you to keep things in life in perspective. In the fast-paced life that we currently live in, it is easy to take the good things in life for granted, and even easier to focus on the bad things. Something as simple as an affirmation saying "I am healthy" in the morning is enough to remind you to be grateful for the good things in your life.

- The practice of daily affirmations and quotes can allow for you to gain mental freedom. You begin to move through the day differently. The things that use to be a bother to you are no longer seem too important. You might also begin to venture into new things that you never thought you would do.

- Daily affirmations are great for increasing how positive you are. When you are more positive, you are going to notice more of the great things that are happening in your life and welcome more blessings and gifts into your life.

- Like bees are attracted to flowers others will become attracted to you. As you become more positive and happy, other people are going to notice. You are going to find yourself helping others without even trying and seeing that is going to help you to stay even more focused. When you have the gift to be an inspiration to others you will continue to affirm your success.

When we can visualize our goals, you are a third of the way to achieving your dream. A vision is something that's internal and special. It is something that is personally given to you. While the destination may be in common with others your journey is specific and unique. There is no two journeys in life that are identical. When faced with achieving a goal no matter what it is you must have a few things that are parallel to you achieving your destination.

First, you must have a clear mindset of what you want. There would be a fault in your destination if you are not clear on exactly what you want to achieve. Secondly, you have to be sure that this is what you want. Being indecisive is a negative variable when trying to achieve a goal. Not being able to go through with anything because you are uncertain if you want to really do it is a waste of time. You must then be able to visualize your goal in its finalization. This is important, when you can see yourself being an entrepreneur, being a doctor, or having lost 50 pounds then this is where the destination becomes more vivid and clear. After doing that you must the go to work! It will be difficult at some point because hey, life happens, but you must be able to push through it in order to continue down your journey. There will be doubts, discouraging moments and sometimes people who will try and deter you from reaching your goals but YOU have to be the one who does not allow for them to take over.

Don't get discouraged if you struggle to eliminate the negative thoughts completely from your mind immediately, it's natural. Simply try to change the negative thought into a positive one. If you can't, just let the negative thought go, recollect your thoughts, and think about something else instead.

Are you ready to get started? Remember to start on day one and do one page a day until you reach the end. In thirty days, you are going to have undergone a complete mental transformation from negative and unhappy to being a positive, happy person on their way to success. Best of luck, enjoy the journey.

Chapter 1: Affirmations – Why They Work and How to Use Them Effectively

"Affirmations are our mental vitamins, providing the supplementary positive thoughts we need to balance the barrage of negative events and thoughts we experience daily." – Tia Walker

It would be so easy for us to toss positive affirmations aside as nothing more than new-age nonsense, a habit that is practiced only by those who are gullible. But there are too many success stories for this and, provided you use them in the right way, you will find that positive affirmations are incredibly powerful, a true aid to success and happiness throughout your life.

Unless you don't have the Internet or the television, you cannot have missed the strong and ever-growing popularity of positive affirmations. They are just about everywhere you look, even on pictures, cups and table coasters. But what are they exactly and why do they work?

What is an Affirmation?

An affirmation is the practice of thinking positively and of empowering yourself. They normally take the form, as you will see throughout this book, of short statements that you must repeat to yourself to create reality in your life. These affirmations are always in the present tense, never past and never future.

While cynical people may choose to write these off as having no meaning, as thoughts that we simply repeat to ourselves instead getting down to the work of making plans for action, affirmations actually play a very big part in the work that you do to mold the career that you want and, provided they are used in the right way, they can help you to get to your destination, taking the right route and with confidence. And, rather than being something we invented just recently, affirmations have been about for a very long time, conceived originally by a man in the medical profession

A Short History of Affirmations

The man who is responsible for affirmations is a French pharmacist and psychologist by the name of Emile Coue. Back in the early twentieth century, he noticed that, when he gave patients a potion and told them, at the same time, just how effective it was, he got better results than with those he said nothing to.

It was then that he realized our minds are constantly occupied by thoughts and that these thoughts became reality, a kind of autosuggestion when he told his patients to repeat these words every day – *"Every day, in every way, I am getting better and better"*. Throughout his work, Coue was responsible for achieving many cures, many of them remarkable, but he also failed in a way as well. He concluded that, if his patients could make an independent judgment about the affirmations they were saying, his methods would not work and his conclusion was that, for an affirmation to work, you have to truly believe it.

Why Not All Affirmations Work

That belief is one of the stumbling points of affirmations. Yes, you can say to yourself repeatedly, "my post-baby career is amazing" but, unless you actually believe that, deep inside of you and with all of your heart, it simply won't work.

You can choose a mantra and you can repeat it every single day but there is no way you can fool the very core of you and if you want your mantra to come true, you must have the deepest of true beliefs in it. Sadly, therefore many people fail with affirmations and I will talk more about this in a later chapter but, we tend to believe that our mantras must be ambitious otherwise there is no point. Dream a big dream or don't dream at all and that is not the way affirmations work.

It is perfectly okay to have a big dream, but when there is no realism in it then it can prove to be a case of 'your reach exceeding your grasp'. We must keep a realistic approach to our goals. Saying that *"I want to go into outer space next year"* and not having a single course on the fundamentals of space under your belt is an unrealistic approach to a big dream. When you have unrealistic goals you are subjecting yourself to vulnerability. If you are unsure of how to set realistic goals no need to worry, I will discuss them later on in this book.

We also make the mistake of looking for affirmations that someone else has come up with, that we can use for our own purposes without really making sure that they work for us. To show you how some affirmations are badly or poorly written, look at these:

- ☐ Saying to yourself, *"I am as thin as a supermodel and well-toned"* isn't going to work when what you see in the mirror is the baby weight you are struggling to shed and you haven't been anywhere near a gym in, well, forever.

- Saying to yourself, *"I am running the most successful multinational company"* won't work if your main way of filling your time through the week is sat down watching television.

- Saying to yourself, *"I am wealthy beyond everything I dreamed of"* won't work if you can't find the money to pay your bills and haven't treated yourself to any new clothes or shoes in months

There is a danger in picking an affirmation that doesn't fit with how you feel and that is that it can make you do the opposite of what you wanted. Instead of a feeling of empowerment and positivity, you end up throwing the towel in, thinking to yourself that where you want to be is so far away from where you are, and you'll never be able to get there so there really isn't any point in trying.

What do you do? Forget your affirmations, throw them all away and go back to how you were. That is absolutely the wrong thing to do. What you must do is pick the right affirmations, or write your own, and use them in the right way.

Finding the Right Affirmation

So, how do you pick the affirmation that is going to work for you? In a lot of ways, it is like a SMART goal:

- **S**pecific

- **M**easured

- **A**chievable

- **R**ealistic

- **T**ime-Related

First, your affirmation must not be vague. Saying something like, *"I have a fantastic career"* isn't really giving your subconscious anything to work with and it is too broad to generate any true conviction. It will also not help you to realize when you have achieved your goal. Instead, you should consider something that is near enough to your situation at the current time to be achievable and realistic. Then find or write an affirmation around it. A couple of examples would be:

- ☐ I enjoy what I do and I am truly appreciated for it
- ☐ I am on a journey that will help me run my own company
- ☐ I respond calmly to stressful situations
- ☐ I am confident and completely at ease in my job interview

These may be slightly above what you are feeling right now because they are describing something that you desire, not something that you cannot attain. They will also let you take the right action for you to achieve them and once you have done that, you move on and come up with a new affirmation for the next big step. Simply match your mantra to your progress, like taking a large project and breaking it down into smaller, more manageable projects.

You must have a sense of certainty of your affirmation, is it something realistic, smart and resourceful? If your affirmation is not achievable, is too ambitious, your core is not going to believe that you can achieve it and that means it will fail.

Create Your Own Personal Affirmations

So, what do you do? Affirmations do work if you use them properly and that means forgetting the one-size-fits-all approach. Yes, you can look for ideas for positive affirmations and, if you find one that fits your situation properly, use it. If not, adapt one or write your own. Tweak existing ones if you need to but make sure they genuinely work for you. Remember: Only **YOU** know what will work for **YOU.**

Chapter 2: Phase One – Days One Through Eight

"We first must think 'I can,' then behave appropriately along that line of thought." – Marsha Sinetar

Since this is your first phase, we are going to make your challenge an easy one. This challenge is something you need to accomplish every day, and not just for this week, but on throughout the entire thirty days.

This phase's challenge has been designed to help you be successful at becoming more positive. Making extra time in your day for new goals can be difficult to do. To help offset that, your challenge this week is going to be to get up a few minutes earlier.

Challenge – Phase One: Set your alarm fifteen minutes earlier than what you are getting up at right now. Use those fifteen minutes every morning to read through that day's affirmation and quote. Take your time reading the affirmation and quote and make sure that you read them more than once.

After you have read the quote a couple of times, close your eyes and think about what the quote means to you. Consider how the quote makes you feel and how you can relate to the quote. If how the quote makes you feel is negative, take a note of that and see if you can find a more positive way to frame your feelings.

Each day is also going to have some things that you can take into consideration to help you get started with the thinking process. As you consider each quote and affirmation, feel free to make notes and jot down any thoughts that you connect to them.

Write the affirmation down somewhere that you are going to see it throughout the day. Whether that means that you are going to email it to yourself, write it on a sticky note and place it on your computer or put it on your phone, make sure it is accessible and visible.

Keep three or four of the affirmations in this book together where you can recite them twice a day. You aren't going to want to have more than three or four to recite a day as this is going to create additional mental stress. Choose the ones that you feel apply the most to your life as the ones that you are going to recite to yourself. You can change which ones you are reciting each day as you wish to.

Day One

Quote: "You can achieve anything you want in life if you have the courage to dream it, the intelligence to make a realistic plan, and the will to see that plan through to the end." – Sidney A. Friedman

Affirmation: The power is within me. I learn from the past, live in the now and plan the future.

Some Things You Should Consider:

When you have courage, you empower yourself to go after something that you may not have any prior knowledge about. Courageous people have often become immortalized throughout history. Courage doesn't come only in the form of wars and battles but can come from personal situations. It takes courage to realize that there is something in your life that you want to change. It takes even more courage to come to the conclusion of beginning to take steps towards what you want to change. When you are courageous you are opening so many links to new opportunities and adventures. Let's be truthful, being courageous is not always easy. Sometimes it can be downright brutal, but it is necessary when the evolution of something is involved. Courage comes from some one having a made-up mind on a circumstance or a situation and finally saying "enough is enough." Only then does true courage come into play, and results are soon to follow.

Many people often correlate the words *intelligent* and *smart* together when in all actuality they are very different. A person can be smart but lack intelligence and a person can be intelligent and not so smart. Do not confuse the two words, you need both to become accomplished.

However, being intellectual is something that you are born with and being smart is something that you learn throughout life. When facing a new situation it is important to gather as much information that you can on the subject matter. This is called being educated, once you have gained education then you are able to apply what you have accumulated to whatever specifics are required. When you are smart you make the best of whatever kind of situation you are faced with. You give it your best and you are also giving your best to the people who are surrounding you. You are showing all of your best attributes: how you verbally communicate, the body language that you give, or your expressiveness. An intelligent individual is someone whose sense of awareness be it for environmental or internal stimulus is quickly absorbed.

Willpower is within all of us. Just like young children who are tempted to eat candy after they have been told not to. It is something that gives us the urge to have a persistent drive. Doing what we want to do whenever we want to do it. Although all of that can sound very empowering but to have an uncontrolled willpower can prove to be a problem when going through life.

Willpower and self-control work hand in hand. There are some things that we really want to do but then have to remove ourselves and our emotions from the situation and ask ourselves "Is this really good for me?" and then attempt to make the best judgment. The key to having great willpower is to have optimum self-control. We all need to practice having self-control as difficult as it may be it can and will keep you from setting your own self back. Self-control is also something that must be practiced over and over again for as you know temptations surround us all every day. The moment that you begin to feel like you are losing self-control is the time to take for personal reflection. Where do you want to be in life? Are the decisions you are making going to impact your goals in a negative way? If so, how should you go about changing your way of thinking to persevere in terms of your aspirations?

People do have differences when it comes to defining what being accomplished is. Some feel that being accomplished is having lots of money, having the "perfect" body or the best relationship. While there are so many definitions, only one has carried so much meaningfulness. It is that being accomplished encompasses the sense of success as a result of preparation and training.

While you are thinking about this quote and repeating this affirmation, think about the things in your life that you want to accomplish. Dreams that you haven't pursued because you feel like you won't accomplish them. Think about the challenges you have overcome in the past.

Say this affirmation like you mean it and believe it. Before you go to bed tonight, stand in front of the mirror and look yourself in the eyes. Repeat today's affirmation and tell yourself you are going to be a better person after these thirty days. Continue telling yourself that you are going to be a better person at the end of this thirty days.

Day Two

Quote: "Man often becomes what he believes himself to be. If I keep on saying to myself that I cannot do a certain thing, it is possible that I may end by really becoming incapable of doing it. On the contrary, if I have the belief that I can do it, I shall surely acquire the capacity to do it even if I may not have it at the beginning." — Mahatma Gandhi

Affirmation: I choose to find hopeful and optimistic ways to look at this.

Some Things You Should Consider:

At a certain point, we all should realize that we are our best advocate. There is no one that can do as much as you can do for yourself. When we have a strong belief that we are capable of doing anything with the right tools we can become unstoppable in this world.

When you are thinking about this quote, consider what you believe yourself to be. If you find yourself using negative words to describe yourself, try to replace as many as those negative ideas with a positive twist on them. If you still find difficulty blocking out those negative thoughts one thing I find helpful is to write down on one side of paper ALL of the things that you dislike or want to change about yourself and on the opposite side write ALL of the things you absolutely love about yourself. When you look at the things you dislike think about the things you want to change about them and how to go about that change. What are some things you need to cut out from your daily life to achieve this change? What is a realistic timeframe that you want to give yourself in order to ensure an achievable destination?

Anytime you are faced with a struggle, repeat the affirmation above. Whether this is a personal struggle, a work struggle, or a financial struggle, this affirmation is going to help you through it. After you have repeated this affirmation when you are struggling for a while, you are going to find yourself naturally looking for a more optimistic approach to a situation without having to give it any thought.

Day Three

Quote: "Once Your Mindset changes, everything on the outside will change along with it." – Steve Maraboli

Affirmation: I clearly see the beauty of life that flourishes around me

Some Things You Should Consider:

While you are thinking about this quote, consider how you look at things. Consider whether you are the kind of person who sees beauty in things or notices the ugliness around them. If you are the kind of person who sees the ugliness, think about how you can see the beauty around you instead. Begin to empathize to the conclusion that there is beauty and wisdom in every situation, whether good or bad. There is always something that we can take away from situations, even if it is not our own.

Having a highly effective mindset makes the best out of any and every kind of situation. It enjoys being in that open space, that present feeling and moment. When you have a passion for something it's almost impossible not to put all of your heart into it. Having a, well, effective mindset will connect that inner drive and the physicality needed to make it your goals real. When your mind is effective the small things that use to be bothersome are no longer. You begin to have a filter of what is important in life and what isn't. You will be able to remain focused on the things that are important along with having the discipline to carry them out. With the effective mindset, you hold the key to opening any of the doors that have been closed in your past, present, and future.

You may ask where or how to start building this *effective mindset*? Well, simple, you can start right now. There are a few ways to begin to build a healthier mindset. To begin, when we can think positively and are able to filter out all of the bad emotions from the past we can then begin to build a healthy mindset. By identifying your negative thoughts and feelings through having awareness. There are tons of cognitive awareness exercises out there that can assist you with this. Once you have an awareness of your thoughts then you can move on to the art of expression.

Expressing the thoughts that we have, whether happy, sad, mad or all in between are extremely important of having thoughtful awareness. By all means get creative. You can journal, dance, paint, scream, meditate or really anything that is a healthy gateway for you to express yourself and everything that might be bottled up on the inside. The moment that you begin to think negative thoughts is the time to refocus your thoughts and put your attention on the positive things about you or the positive things going on around you. Lastly, use your imagination! Imagery is so important in everyday life and it plays such a huge role in the way that we perceive the world. Try imagining yourself in a better place be it physically, financially, emotionally or mentally.

While you go about your day today, consider all the amazing things that are around you. From the flower growing in the garden to the bird flying overhead, there is beauty in all things, when you can see the beauty in these things you are going to be able to accomplish more.

Day Four

Quote*:* "The true secret of happiness lies in taking a genuine interest in all the details of daily life." – William Morris

Affirmation*:* For me, happiness is a journey, not a destination. I have been blessed with happiness, and my journey is endless.

What motivates you? Take a few minutes to really evaluate your answer. Do you get out of the bed because you have to, want to or need to? When you are on your morning, mid-day, and evening commutes, are you satisfied with what you are doing? What is it you are doing all of this for? When you are faced with these questions and you have all negative answers then it is time to re-evaluate what is keeping you in order to be doing the same things that are bringing you displeasure.

To be quite frank, life is too short to be doing something that you are not happy doing. In the terms of occupation, there are thousands if not millions who absolutely hate the occupation that they are currently in. The saving grace is that can be *changed*. You do not have to stick to a job that you do not love, while it is a great idea to have a backup plan before just putting in a resignation letter, there is nothing that makes you stay somewhere where you are not fulfilled.

When seeking motivation you should always take into consideration what it is that *you* want. Motivation should not come from someone else, it should come from you. When we are truly motivated to do something we withhold all prejudices and give it 100% every time and we are purely happy to do it.

Some Things You Should Consider:

The greatest journey that we all will ever be on is a simple word called *life*. Consider the parts of your day that bring you the most happiness. Is it when you wake up in the morning? Going for a quiet walk on a hiking trail? Drinking some delicious coffee? What is it about those parts of your day that make you happy? Think about the things that are all around you during those parts of the day. Consider the people, the noise levels, the smells, tastes and anything else that is within your surroundings. Take note of all of those details and commit them to your memory. These details will help you retain the good feelings associated with those experiences and remind you that at that specific moment in time there was a moment of bliss.

Day Five

Quote: "Happiness lies in the joy of achievement and the thrill of creative effort" – Franklin D. Roosevelt

Affirmation: Happiness is a choice. I base my happiness on my accomplishments and the blessings I've been given.

Some Things You Should Consider:

"He makes me happy."

"She makes me happy."

Have you ever heard anyone say those lines? My guess would be absolutely. In some form or another, we have always tried to associate our own personal happiness with the involvement of something or someone outside of our own self. This is not how happiness is developed or executed. The idea of having to chase after the emotion of happiness, an emotion that comes from nowhere but within, has been the downfall of so many people and has easily contributed to seeking validation from others. One must then ask themselves, "What is needed for me to be happy?" Take a minute or two and ask yourself what you think is needed in order for you to be happy.

Understand that no one can make you happy, though there are experiences that bring the emotion of happiness into margin but it's only received if you are open to the delivery. True happiness is personal and direct. Consider the things you have done in your life that make you happy. Think about the people in your life, and the goals you have accomplished that contribute to bring about your happiness. Realize that even when you weren't successful, the excitement of trying brought you happiness as well. There are going to be failures throughout life's journey, and that's okay, but it is up to you to disallow or allow for them to have a direct impact on you and how you are continuing throughout life.

Anytime you find yourself feeling unhappy with the hand life has dealt you, repeat the affirmation above and remember, happiness is a choice.

Day Six

Quote: "Progress is impossible without change and those who cannot change their minds cannot change anything" – George Bernard Shaw

Affirmation: I have been given endless talents which I begin to utilize today.

Some Things You Should Consider:

Progress is often understood as a business term, while it is most suitable for any business person to use in their endeavors it is a term that should be used in self-motivation and self-help. Having progress means that you have started from somewhere and you are advancing into something grander. Progress is the motion in-between ground zero and the finalization of a goal. In order to have progress, you must have productivity. What are you doing in your day to day living that is showing a direct progression to your goals and achievements?

If you find your answer to be in the negative aspect then my suggestions would be finding and applying steps to progression. Some of the steps may include:

    -Know what makes *you you*. What do you do well? What are some of your favorite things to do on your down time? What are some things about your life that you want to change?

    -Create a plan and know how to manage what your goals are. When you know what your goals are you create different strategies to help you strengthen those pieces of your life that will make you getting your goals.

    - Be aware of what your setbacks are. When you are aware of the bad habits you practice you realize how much of it is a part of your life.

Ever hear the quote "*You are what you eat*"?, well here's another one for you to remember "*You are what you think*". If you want to progress towards a happier life, you are going to have to change how you are thinking about things. This isn't as hard as it seems. While you are thinking about this quote, consider opinions or habits you have that you are unwilling to change. While thinking about them, are there any of these things that have proven to have a negative outcome? If so, is it something you can be comfortable living with for the rest of your life?

Anytime you find yourself in a situation that cannot be solved in the usual way, think about the affirmation above and remember that you are capable of change, if you just utilize your talents and find a new solution. Interpersonal change usually doesn't happen overnight and it may not even happen over a week, it takes time so don't rush.

Day Seven

Quote: "Don't rely on someone else for your happiness and self-worth. Only you can be responsible for that. If you can't love and respect yourself – no one else will be able to make that happen. Accept who you are – completely; the good and the bad – and make changes as YOU see fit – not because you think someone else wants you to be different." – Stacey Charter

Affirmation: I love and respect myself as I am.

Some Things You Should Consider:

This society has proven to be a place where being accepted by others should be the number one priority of the day. We put out everything we do on social media. We dress to impress! We try and keep up with the "*Who's who..*". Why? While you are thinking about the quote above, consider how much you rely on other people to validate you. Are you confident in who you are, or do you need other people to give you positive affirmations to feel like you are worthwhile?

Only you can make you happy. No one in this world has the capability to do that. Seeking validation from others only allows for them to gain control and for you to lose control. It shouldn't matter what others think of you. Be the best you that you can be and anyone else's opinion should fall irrelevant, especially if it is negative.

The world we live in is all about representation, how a person presents them self is the number one judgment of character by others. The way you dress, the way you speak, or the way you look has a direct impact on how others will treat you. This is an unfortunate reality for many people, especially as young children are being more and more impacted of the idea of "image" and are sometimes willing to go to extremes to have their "image" protected. Self-esteem for adolescents and adults alike are often tangible according to our interactions with others.

When you have good self-esteem you have good self-values. When a person has good self-esteem they have a wonderful collective opinion about themselves - how they look, how they speak, their style and everything else! They view themselves as nothing less than great and they don't allow for others beliefs or opinions to impact them in a negative way. Your confidence level will increase drastically and you will find yourself being more comfortable and open with new opportunities and adventures. When you have high self-esteem you demand respect from others and give respect to others all because you have the highest respect for yourself. You also have true freedom and can openly and happily be yourself.

If you are struggling with having high self-esteem then there are some practices that you can try to heighten those emotions. You can begin with encouraging and complimenting yourself. Whenever you have made a mistake forgive yourself and forgive the people who have done wrong to you. I know that this may be very difficult but when we allow the hurt and pain another person has caused us to be unforgiven we are giving our power to that situation and this can be very draining to the mind, body, and spirit.

"The greatest thing in the world is to know how to belong to oneself."

-Michel de Montaigne, The Complete Essays

Having self-worth and self-values are essential in having a high self-esteem. When you have high standards about what you allow to enter into your life and your mind, you have the ultimate control on how situations cycle. If you know that there are some people in your life who tend to be a bit on the narcissistic side and they tend to bring you down then it will be easier to cut them out of your inner life when you have raised your standards. We should never settle for anyone or anything that goes directly against what we feel we deserve and our on moral character.

There are two types of influences: good and bad. The difficulty comes when we are naturally given the gift to have freedom of choice. The closer something is to you the greater of an influence it will have, if allowed. It is always a good idea to surround yourself with positive influences. These can really be in great variation as we are all drawn to different things. The key to being well influenced is to keep the bad influences far away! It is sometimes difficult to avoid the presence of a bad influence because they are indeed everywhere, but the wonderful news is that a bad intention sticks out like a sore thumb. *Misery loves company,* and it will do anything to have others join the party. If you are wise enough you can see someone who has a toxicity that would not be good for you to be around. When you are aware of this then it is easy for you to remove yourself from that situation.

Say this affirmation to yourself as often as you can, until you truly believe it. You cannot become more positive, happier or successful if you don't first love, respect and accept yourself for who you are.

Day Eight

Quote: "Work hard for what you want because it won't come to you without a fight. You must be strong and courageous and know that you can do anything you put your mind to. If somebody puts you down or criticizes you, just keep on believing in yourself and turn it into something positive." – Leah LaBelle

Affirmation: Giving up is easy, and always an option so I will delay it for another day.

Some Things You Should Consider:

Many things that come easy usually are not all that legit. If you ever recall getting a great deal on something and then after just a few uses it begins to give you some problems and soon after just doesn't work out altogether. That is a wonderful example of things that are cheap aren't necessarily good. There is the triangle often used by builders and designers, you can have something good, fast, or cheap. The trouble is you can only choose two of those options. If its good and fast, it won't be cheap. Cheap and good, it won't be fast. I think you're getting my point. So it is for going through life and climbing to your goals and aspirations. There is a lot of hard work that is required in order to get to a destination, sometimes decades worth. You have to be real with yourself and ask if that is something that you are okay with, being in something for the long haul because that is what you truly want.

When we have worked hard for something the passion is slowly kneaded into the pathway and we begin to have an appreciation for not only the hard work that we have done, but we appreciate ourselves even more for going through it. This increases our self-worth and it is such a great feeling. Remember that hard work never goes without being rewarded in the end. Whether your reward is something of the physical world or emotional, hard work pays off.

We must remember to teach others the value of hard work, especially our youth. It is important for them to know that nothing in life is promised and that there are sacrifices that must be made at some point in their lives. Equipping them with the knowledge of hard work will help them in so many ways.

Do not forget to be your biggest motivator, nothing will ever get done in your life unless you make it up in your mind that you need it and want it to come to pass. Anytime you find yourself struggling to motivate yourself to do something, say the affirmation above out loud. Remember, real strength shows itself when you don't quit, and you see something through to the ending. Not only does it build strength but it also builds character and many more wonderful attributes to you own self.

You have made it to the end of the first phase. Congratulations for making it this far. Consider how your thoughts have changed in the last week. Are you beginning to see things in a more positive way? Are you finding that you are happier and feeling more fulfilled?

Success Story – Thomas

"There is nothing in the world that I cannot achieve when I have the courage to believe."

– Chiara Gizzi

My name is Thomas, I am not quite 50 yet and I have been using positive affirmations for more than 20 years, almost constantly. Sometimes they have taken my life over and have delved into my pursuits in the biggest ways possible but to me, this is a good thing. Affirmations have given me the opportunity to transform myself in the most positive ways and have helped me on my way to accomplishing many goals.

It all began when I started to use affirmations to improve my confidence levels. When I started, I was 17 years old, shy, didn't find it very easy to make friends and I would as good as run from a girl! Within just a few days of using affirmations, I began to see a major difference in my thoughts, about how I saw myself, how is thought about happiness, my self-esteem, and positivity. Over the following weeks, everything changed for me and I was hooked – affirmations became my life. I was more outgoing and confident than I had ever been before, I found it easier to make friends and started socializing – and I started talking to girls!

This was just the start though and over the next 20 or so years, my day has begun, without fail, with 5 minutes of positive affirmations and, every day, the last thing at night, I repeat those affirmations into the bathroom mirror. Not a day has passed when I have not done this and the transformation has been remarkable.

What did I use affirmations for? Just about anything you can think of. They helped me to lose weight and start taking exercise on a regular basis. They pushed me into working hard at running and at sports. I used them to help me in my hobbies, to boost myself when I was down and to get the right mindset for running my real estate properties and my businesses. I also used them as a way of helping to boost my personal relationships and live life.

After spending the last 20 or so years running my own businesses I have now been able to take early retirement although I do keep my hand in with some business interests and personal projects. And I still do my affirmations, every single morning and night. Throughout my life, throughout all the changes, the ups, the downs, affirmations have been there for me and they can be there for you too.

Chapter 3: Phase Two – Days Nine Through Fourteen

"Thousands of candles can be lighted from a single candle, and the life of the candle will not be shortened. Happiness never decreases by being shared." – Buddha

You've made it to phase two! How did you do over the last week? Take a moment to consider how you did with the first challenge so far. Do you feel that starting your day with a quote and affirmation changed how you approached your day? Consider how you are feeling daily. Would you say that you can feel yourself becoming progressively more positive?

At this point, getting up a little earlier each day should be becoming a habit and a normal part of your routine. Remember that you are going to continue getting up early and committing that time to reflecting on the quote and daily affirmation of the day throughout the rest of the thirty days. You should also have a few affirmations that mean something to you that you are saying each day.

This phase's challenge is based on the quote above. Sharing happiness is a great way to bring more happiness to you, and when you see yourself bring happiness to others, you will be amazed at how great it makes you feel.

Challenge – Phase Two: Your challenge this phase is to spread a little happiness every day. This can mean anything you want it to. You can take a minute out of your day to call someone who you know would appreciate hearing from you. You can take a minute to thank the grocery store clerk for being kind. It could also mean surprising someone with a cup of coffee or a treat. Any form of gratitude or positivity is going to go a long way towards bringing happiness into other people's lives. When you see how happy you can make others, you are going to feel happier as well.

The reason that you feel happy when you make other people happy is that we can empathize the emotions that we observe in others. In the 1960's a Dutch Scientist, Christian Huygens discovered that if he hung multiple pendulums on the wall, they would all end up swinging in perfect synchrony. This proved to be true even if he set them in motion at different times. This happens in human beings as well. You have probably noticed that when someone is in a bad mood, that bad mood can be passed on to others. The same is true for happiness.

By spreading happiness to others not only do you gain the same emotion but they also have to capacity to now spread it to others and before you know it there is an overflow and what seems to be an endless chain reaction of happiness.

Day Nine

Quote: "There is only one way to happiness, and that is to cease worrying about things which are beyond the power of our will." – Epictetus

Affirmation: Happiness is my birthright. I choose to be happy, and I deserve to be happy.

Some Things You Should Consider:

While you are thinking about the quote above, consider all the things that you are worried about that are sacrificing your happiness. Is there anything you can do to control those things? Or are they beyond your control? For the things that are beyond your control, consider what you can do help reduce your worry about the things that are beyond your control.

Imagine a bag on your back, this bag holds every situation you ever have worried about; think on how heavy that bag is now? Is it just about to weigh you down? When we worry and continue to hold on to emotional baggage we are putting tremendous tension and weight on our mind. When our minds are down we are incapable of working to our fullest potential. I know, it is easier said than done, but when we worry about things that are out of our control it begins to control everything about us. We end up not functioning so well and this can then jeopardize our health and wellbeing.

The number one killer of humans is stress and the diseases brought about by stress. Stress is like a leech that feeds on every part of the human. It feeds on our minds, our bodies and our spirits. Fortunately, this can be managed through lifestyle alterations. Proper diet, expression, and exercises for the mind and body do wonders for someone who is trying to eliminate the feeling of stress. If there is a situation or a job that is more stressful than enjoyable and you find that it is too much, my advice would be to find something else that brings you peace and joyfulness.

Anytime you come across a situation that is decreasing your happiness, repeat the affirmation above. Remember, you deserve to be happy, and you can make the choice to be happy.

Day Ten

Quote: "It's not the events of our lives that shape us, but our beliefs as to what those events mean." – Tony Robbins

Affirmation: I always spot opportunities and utilize them. New doors are always opening for me.

Some Things You Should Consider:

Reading the above quote, can you think of some times in your life when you felt that you were being shaped by the things that were happening around you? What was shaping you, was it the event itself or how you were reacting to the event?

Many people consider themselves to be a victim of circumstance when it is an internal decision to allow the circumstance to define them. How can you change how you are viewing those circumstances?

Bad things are going to happen, but it is what you do once the bad thing has happened that counts. You just miss a flight to an important event, what do you do? Do you just quit and return home or do you try and reconcile the problem? There are always going to be moments in life when you think to yourself, "Can anything ever go right in my life?". The answer is yes but you have to also realize that bad things are a part of life and there is no way of getting around it. You have to just take things as they come to you and handle them in the most positive way you possibly can. If not, then you will shut yourself out of personal growth and opportunities.

There is also something called the Law of Attraction which an entire book can be written on but I will sum it up a little. When we put out the thought that something bad is going to happen then we are holding up a sign for all of the bad events that we are thinking about to come directly into our midst. We have to watch how we think and what we think. Some of the bad thoughts we have are a gateway for them to become our living reality. Whenever you think about something bad that is going to happen to you try are redirect your thoughts into a positive one.

For example, instead of saying "*I am going to get into a wreck.*" Try saying something like, "*I am going to have a safe and wonderful drive.*" This sends out the energy of attracting a good and safe journey versus attracting destruction and discord.

The above affirmation is a great one when you feel as though you are being limited by your circumstances. New opportunities are always opening themselves up to you, and there are always new opportunities for you to explore.

Day Eleven

Quote: "Action is the foundational key to all success" – Pablo Picasso

Affirmation: I am solution oriented. All problems are solvable.

Some Things You Should Consider:

When you consider the quote above, remember that the foundation of anything is the most important thing. When you are building a house, the house is only as strong as the foundation. The quote tells us that actions are the foundation for success. If you aren't taking any action, you aren't going to accomplish any success.

Action sometimes requires sacrifice. If your goal is weight loss then you have to watch how much and what you consume on an 'around the clock' basis. Sacrifice is not an easy thing especially when you are used to doing something you like or love. However, if you have a goal you're striving to achieve whether it's health, financial, or personal sometimes there will be huge sacrifices that must be made.

If you have felt as though you are stuck in a rut recently, and feel as though there is no way to move forward in your life, this affirmation is exactly what you are going to need to help you through it. Repeat this affirmation to yourself as often as you can. Remember, if you are looking for the solution, you are going to find it.

Recall earlier in this book when I stated that there would be some keys on how to build realistic goals. It is very important to set realistic goals for yourself, to promote healthy endurance and strive. Here are a few points to keep in mind when setting a realistic goal:

    1. Keep a visual representation of your goals. When we see something with our eyes multiple times it begins to make a fingerprint in our mind and this is very helpful when it comes to affirmations. You can write on whatever you like, a mirror, the wall, make a screensaver on your phone or computer, on poster board. Pretty much anything that you will see multiple times a day.

    2. Having smaller goals within a larger one. This helps to keep you motivated and moving in the right direction. Set up small milestones on your journey.

3. Keep your goals uncomplicated. Be specific and upfront. State how you are going to go about achieving your goal.

Example:

<u>Make Better Grades</u> vs. <u>Make Better Grades By</u>

Studying 30mins 4X Daily

Going to Study Sessions

Asking Specific Questions

4. Measure your progress. If your goal is an increase in financial gain, see how your track of expenses have declined or inclined over all of your income.

When we take action on our goals we are adding the nutrient that is required for our dream to take root and grow. Actions are something that can be both voluntary and involuntary. When you put forth a good action then you will involuntarily receive action back. You may have the question of how to take action? The first thing is to have a reality check. What is your mindset focused on at the present time? You have to reconnect yourself with your thoughts and feelings. Once you have done that set your priorities in line. If you are in charge of governing over something or others then you have to be accountable and make yourself available. You then must hold yourself responsible for your actions and the outcome of your situation. You are the mastermind here and you are ultimately in control of how your life will and does play out. Set your own standards and principles on how you want things to go and try your best to not stray away from it. Lastly don't be too serious, when we are hard on ourselves or others it tends to take the enjoyment out of the circumstance. No one wants to be around someone who is always controlling and can never seem to lighten up.

These are all some positive ways to begin to take action in your life and your career. These things will assist in building great characteristics and moral.

Day Twelve

Quote: "Optimism is the faith that leads to achievement. Nothing can be done without hope and confidence." – Helen Keller

Affirmation: I am confident, and I am capable. There is no challenge I cannot overcome.

Some Things You Should Consider:

What is your definition of hope? What are some of the things you feel you are the most confident in? As the quote states about nothing in life can be done if we are not hopeful and confident. The whole idea behind wishing is the thought that hope and strong desire will bring whatever you want right into our lives. A wish is given usually when the situation seems very unpredictable and unobtainable. Hope is the belief that something can certainly happen, it is faith.

We have to believe in what we dream of, there is nothing more important in building ourselves up and moving throughout life. Empowerment of what you want through hope and optimism is what will keep you motivated and your dreams fresh.

Think about the situations that you are the most optimistic. What are the times that you are the most confident that you are going to be able to achieve your goals? What situations are you the least confident in?

When we have high confidence it empowers us to be our best, do our best, and think our best. Some may experience a heightened sense of euphoria and adrenaline.

Whenever you are in doubt of your abilities, repeat the affirmation above. Place it next to your bathroom mirror, seeing it on a regular basis is going to help you believe it even more. Of all the affirmations that we have gone over this far, this is the one that you need to believe in the most.

Day Thirteen

Quote: "To carry a positive action, we must develop here a positive vision – Dalai Lama

Affirmation: I am going to help others. I have enough happiness inside me to share.

Some Things You Should Consider:

When you read the quote above, what is the very first thought that comes to your mind? Can you think of a time when you were expecting a negative outcome and it came true? What about a time when you were expecting a positive vision and the positive vision can true? Often, when you can envision the outcome being positive, you are more likely to get that positive outcome.

There is some truth to the laws of attraction, and we can sometimes be our worse enemy. People often expect the worst in a foreign situation and tell themselves that they are expecting the worst, so they shouldn't be disappointed when it happens right? However, they are still just as disappointed when their negative vision comes to fruition. Don't get caught up in that trap. When you think negative things are going to happen, they are more likely going to happen. Instead of thinking the worst out of a situation you are faced with try turning it around into a happier situation, think of something beautiful you can take away from it.

Having optimism through your everyday existence is what allows you to keep an open mind and an open heart. Believing in something far from what you can see gives you the inspiration to keep moving forward.

How are you doing on this phases' challenge? Are you finding it easy to bring happiness into other people's lives? If you are finding the challenge to be difficult, repeat the above affirmation to yourself. There is happiness inside you, and when you choose to share it with others, it comes back to you tenfold.

Day Fourteen

Quote: "You'll never find a rainbow if you're looking down" — Charlie Chaplin

Affirmation: I am kind, I am loving, I am happy.

Some Things You Should Consider:

Take time to think about what the quote above means. Think about a goal that you are trying to reach. Are you on the right path to meet that goal? If you aren't on the right path to reach your goals, you are never going to get to them. Take some time to analyze where you are in life and where you want to go. What changes can you make?

It is important to remember that no matter what kind of journey you are on you have to ensure yourself and make the most important person in your journey yourself. When there are rough patches in life you can feel alone, sad or like you aren't getting anywhere but know that after every dark storm comes wonderful sunlight.

Be inspired by the things that surround you. Anything and everything that we come in contact can have some type of meaning to it. Sometimes things can come into our life for a reason and a season and it is up to us to recognize it and take what we need from it. There are many lessons that can be learned in every moment of the day.

No matter how far you are from the path you want to be on, you can still be happy with where you are. Remind yourself that you are a kind and loving person. Happiness is a choice you can make. If you aren't happy at this moment, only you can change that. Repeat the affirmation above and remind yourself of all the reasons you have to be happy.

Success Story – Whitney

"All is well. Everything is working out for my highest good. Out of this situation, only good will come. I am safe." – Louise L. Hay

My name is Whitney and, in the middle of the eighties, I was given a book, a book that I still must this day. My parents had been divorced for a few years and, although things were good, it was tough at a time when divorce want really all that common. A friend of my mother gave me this book, the Rainbow Heart Book, called "You Can heal Your Life" by Louse L Hay. And I must say that, since that time, my life has been one hell of a journey!

This brand-new book seemed to fit with me, being the kid of divorced parents at my school. Every exercise that was in it, I savored, just to get to know every different aspect of the me that I am. I wanted to be a better person, more accepting, more whole and I learned that I was a loving person, a lovable person and that I was loved, not just by me but by the entire universe – and I still am to this day.

Out of all the techniques in this book, the one that inspired me the most and has stuck with me is affirmations. It is these that I thank for the fact that I became a happy teenager, a confident one, one who was happy to be herself and not trying to be something others wanted me to be.

For me, an affirmation is everything and anything that I think, that I say, that I believe, experience and feel. Affirmations have become me, they reflect me and they are me.

So many people use negative self-talk and this is what drives their affirmations, drawing them into negativity that they really didn't want. It started like this for me but I learned to move my focus and use my affirmations for a more positive life and it is these positive affirmations that have seen me through many an uphill struggle.

When I was in my twenties, my dad passed on, completely unexpectedly and that changed my whole life forever. I got stuck in a grief rut – Í release myself as I do in each moment, free of self-judgment"

Later on, in my twenties, I was diagnosed with cancer and, as it does with just about everyone who is diagnosed, it stole my breath, it stunned me. I stumbled through wondering why this was happening, what had I done? At this point, my affirmations became passionate – "I am living my life to the full, treasuring every single day as it comes"

When I was in my thirties, I became unfulfilled with my job, I wasn't happy or satisfied with what I was doing. I felt as if I was overworked, ill because of stress and burned out. My affirmations changed – Í am living my purpose in life, engaging my Sacred Gifts for the healthy benefit of me and others around me"

Today, I am that happy smiling person I was back in twelfth grade and I put that down to my belief in affirmations and the fact that I have made them a part of my daily life, especially the most important one of all – "I am truly grateful"

You are halfway done!

Congratulations on making it to the halfway point of the journey. Many try and give up long before even getting to this point, so you are to be congratulated on this. You have shown that you are serious about getting better every day. I am also serious about improving my life and helping others get better along the way. To do this I need your feedback. Click on the link below and take a moment to let me know how this book has helped you. If you feel there is something missing or something you would like to see differently, I would love to know about it. I want to ensure that as you and I improve, this book continues to improve as well. Thank you for taking the time to ensure that we are all getting the most from each other.

Chapter 4: Phase Three – Days Fifteen Through Twenty-Two

"You cannot change what happens to you but you can control your attitude towards what happens to you, and in that, you will be mastering change rather than allowing it to master you." – Brian Tracy

You are still coming back every day and reading another page in this book, and you have made it to phase three.

How do you feel you did with making other people happy in the last phase? Did you notice that making other people happy had the power to increase how you were feeling? I encourage you to continue to go out of your way to do things for others that are going to make them happy, even though it is no longer a part of your challenge.

This week's challenge is a little different than the last two weeks. This week your challenge is going to be about change. You've already been working on changing your mindset and your attitude, even if you didn't realize you were. This week we are going to take that one step further. This challenge is also going to give you a lead into your week four challenge.

Challenge – Phase Three: Your challenge this phase is going to center around making changes. For each day this phase, you are going to make a list of something good that happened, something bad that happened, and something positive that can come from the bad thing that happened. Finding something positive out of a negative is a difficult challenge, but it is an important part of finding success and happiness.

Don't worry; I am not going to send you into this challenge without any education on how you can best find the positive in a negative situation. Here are some tips to help you with this process:

1. Identify Your Emotions – Sometimes this can be a bit of a challenge, especially if it involves something unpleasant. If you can label the emotion you are feeling in a negative situation; you can get a better handle on the situation. This is because you will be able to tell what emotions are skewing your interpretation of the situation.

2. Find A Lesson – Experience has always proven to be the best teacher. There is a lesson in every situation. If you work hard to find the lesson, you are more likely to see the positive in a situation.

3. Look For The Benefit – Sometimes when you find yourself in a negative situation, there is something small that you are going to gain a benefit. This could be something like a free cup of coffee after receiving the wrong order at the coffee shop or trying a new dish when the restaurant ran out of an ingredient that is necessary for your usual. In both situations, you can choose to dwell on the negative aspect of the situation, and indeed, they would seem to be a big deal to some people. However, you also have the choice to focus on the compensation the coffee shop gave you or the fantastic new dish you experienced.

Use these tips to help you change the view of some of your experiences this week from negative to positive.

Day Fifteen

Quote: "To create more positive results in your life, replace 'if only' with 'next time'." – Celestine Chua

Affirmation: There is a great reason this is unfolding before me now.

Some Things You Should Consider:

Have it made up in your mind that failure is <u>not</u> an option for you. Write it down on sticky notes and post it everywhere in your house. The more you see it, the more you hear it, the more you will feel it and then you will live it. When things get rough it's okay to seek help and assistance from resources that have truly good intentions and will provide as being a great influence in helping you to make the best decision for your situations.

Sometimes we tend to dwell in the past, and the past should be left exactly where it is supposed to be. We should take what we need from the past to help us continue to evolve into the person we are destined to become and learn from the mistakes. This is not always very easy but it is the best thing that you can do for yourself. When we learn to let go and recognize that we are human and being human is not an easy journey but we can do it through perseverance and learning who we really are and accepting things.

When things are not going the way you want them to in your life, think about how you typically respond. If you find that you are often responding in a helpless manner, this quote is exactly what you need to think about. Instead of feeling helpless, consider the things you would do differently if you were in the same situation again.

The affirmation above is great for reminding you that everything happens for a reason. Sometimes good things happen, and sometimes bad things happen. Sometimes that reason is clear and other times it isn't. When you feel like you aren't able to identify the reason that something in your life is happening, repeat this quote to yourself as often as you can until you have been able to find positive reasons for the situation.

Day Sixteen

Quote: "A pessimist sees the difficulty in every opportunity; an optimist sees the opportunity in every difficulty" – Winston Churchill

Affirmation: I can overcome this challenge. This challenge is going to lead to great things for me.

Some Things You Should Consider:

When you come across a troubling situation it's so easy to see the negative and then give way to doubt but you cannot allow for a gloomy situation to override your journey. Optimism is an overall expectation that there is greatness in everything. When you have made it to the top of a hill you feel a sense of gratification which is due to your own endurance and optimism about how great the outcome would be. It is the same kind of approach that you should have when facing obstacles in your life. Once you have overcome something you have the ability to share your optimistic point of view to someone who might be going through the same series of events.

Reading the quote, try to determine if you are more of an optimist or a pessimist. Keep in mind; it is possible to be both an optimist and a pessimist depending on the situation that you find yourself in. The key is to bring awareness to yourself if you see that you are becoming a pessimist when faced with a situation.

Think about the situations that you find yourself to be pessimistic in. In those situations, is it possible for you to find something positive that you can focus on?

When you find yourself in a position that it is hard to see the positive in, use the affirmation above to remind yourself that you can overcome any challenges and challenges are meant to lead you to new opportunities, if you are open to seeing them.

Day Seventeen

Quote: "We become what we think about" – Earl Nightingale

Affirmation: I am capable of seeing the good in every situation. I am defined by the things I choose to think about.

Some Things You Should Consider:

Though this may seem like an impossible thing to consider, when you are faced with a difficult situation it is important to not think about it too much. When we over-think on negative circumstances we are not able to gain full control of the situation and collectively make a good decision about how to go about handling it. Overthinking can be a bad habit and it can lead to minor setbacks that if gone unchecked can become a detrimental characteristic in your life.

People who overthink on situations can develop sleeping problems because their brain is so wound up with multiple thoughts and feelings that it never is given the proper opportunity to settle down and relax. An over-thinker also tends to overanalyze everything that they come in contact with. The over-thinker often takes the saying *reading between the lines* very far. The feeling of having to control everything is not healthy and can drive you a little crazy at times and can cause other health issues if it goes untreated.

If you suffer from overthinking things here are a few things you can add to your daily routine to help:

- Acknowledge that you are having issues with overthinking every situation.

- Tone down your mind. You can do this by listening to some relaxation tapes or music (I personally enjoy listening to the White Noise genre)

- Baking, putting together a puzzle or whatever relaxes and quiets your mind.

- Take small steps to reset your balance. Since this is a habit it is going to take time to revert from it. It is a transformation.

We have already discussed that your frame of mind is a huge part of what goes on around you, or at least how you perceive it. When considering the quote above,

"We become what we think about," think about the strengths you have and the strengths you would like to have. Think about a negative situation you have been in lately, what good was in that situation? Did you gain wisdom, understanding, or insight?

Using the affirmation above, remind yourself that there is good in every situation, regardless of how negative it seems like the time. Negative situations do not have the ability to define you. Choose to see, and focus, on whatever good you can find in a moment, even if it isn't directly related to the situation.

Day Eighteen

Quote: "Find a place inside where there's joy, and the joy will burn out the pain" – Joseph Campbell

Affirmation: My body is healthy; my mind is brilliant; my soul is tranquil.

Some Things You Should Consider:

There is nothing worse than something taking our joy away… but wait, nothing can just come and take joy, it has to be sacrificed. When we allow things to steal our joy we are hurting ourselves. Just like happiness, joy is an emotion that is personal and direct. No one has the right or should ever be given the privilege to take your joy from you.

Sometimes it can seem as if all the negativity around you is bringing you down and you can't bring yourself above it all. The quote above is a reminder to find the joy that is inside you, regardless of what it is you feel joyous about allowing the joy to outshine the negativity all around you.

When faced with hard times it is important to recollect all your memories of joyous times and allow that to rekindle your joyfulness. When you have joy it should not only be kept in you but also shared. It is the gift that keeps on giving. You never know what will make someone's day, week, or year. By sharing and spreading joy and happiness it surely would make all of our lives a lot easier.

It is my belief that the wealthiest thing to have in life is the ultimate joy. Something that comes only from within yourself, nothing or no one has any role in it. It is just you! The experiences that we go through can be horrible or blissful but if we choose to take the beauty out of it and carry that with us we will always find a center of joy within ourselves.

The affirmation above serves as a reminder that there is always something to be thankful for. Having gratitude for your body, mind, and soul is a great way to show joy and to allow that joy to become your primary focus.

Day Nineteen

Quote*:* "Our greatest weakness lies in giving up. The most certain way to succeed is always to try just one more time." – Thomas A. Edison

Affirmation*:* I see the perfection in all my flaws and all my genius.

Some Things You Should Consider:

Think about the quote above. Can you think of a time that you gave up? What about a situation where you decided to try one more time and that last try was the difference between finding success and being unsuccessful? While it is important to know when to approach a situation from a different angle or to leave a situation and focus your efforts elsewhere, if there is something you truly want the only way you are going to get it is to keep trying.

The definition of perseverance is the steadfastness in doing something despite difficulty or delay in achieving success. When you are faced with difficulty or there is a malfunction in the process of you achieving a goal now is the time to reflect on your definition of perseverance and continue to move forward. Whether by changing your approach or if you should move on to another situation, perseverance is key.

Every part of you is important to who you are. This includes your strengths and your weaknesses. If you try to hide your flaws and only show your strengths, you are not going to be happy, and people aren't going to know you for the real you. Embrace your flaws and weaknesses as a crucial part of your personality. Be honest and upfront with yourself. Use the affirmation above to remind yourself that your flaws aren't necessarily a bad thing, and can be used to your advantage.

When we are knowledgeable about our flaws we then have the capability to go about them in a positive direction for correction. Our flaws and attributes are what makes us unique, some of our flaws can be detrimental to our evolvement and this requires some reflection and admittance in order to change. Our greatest attributes should also be reflected upon because these are the things about us that are positive and keep us at our best, we should never neglect them.

Day Twenty

Quote: "Believe that your life is worth living, and your belief will help create the fact" – William James

Affirmation: I am worth having good things happen to me. I bring happiness into my life.

Some Things You Should Consider:

Do you genuinely feel that your life is worth living? Do you feel like you are making a significant contribution to society, or at the very least to the people who are closest to you?

At some point in every person's life there is time in our lives where we ask ourselves questions like "What is my purpose?" or "Why am I here?". It is a very difficult to answer a question to which you have no answer to give. Everyone has a reason for being here, though it may seem like a cliché of an answer it is in no doubt that we are here for specific reasons.

Somehow we have confused the "rat race" mentality for truly living. While it is important to provide the necessities to sustain life, there are many materialistic things that hold too much power in our lives. When you free yourself from attachments, be it materialistic or other living things, you are opening yourself to a quality life. When you have so many things you must house them be it externally or internally. It is important to let some things go! You will free yourself slowly and surely. In no way am I saying to give up everything in your life that you have but without the clutter of things, people, and places, you and your dreams can grow and blossom.

By using the affirmation above, you can remind yourself that you are worth having good things happening. No one is inherently deserving of having bad things happen to them. The things that happen to us are the things that we have brought into our lives. Remind yourself that you are worth being happiness and that good things can happen to you too, and then look for those good things to begin happening.

Day Twenty-One

Quote: "You can always do more than you think you can" – John Wooden

Affirmation: I am capable of accomplishing whatever I set my mind to.

Some Things You Should Consider:

The quote above serves as a reminder that we all tend to undersell ourselves, especially to ourselves. Think about a time when you gave up on something because you felt as though you could do what you had originally set out to do. Or, perhaps a time when you only did the bare minimum because you didn't feel like you could contribute anything extra to a project. Now think about a time when you pushed yourself further than you thought you were capable of being pushed. How did you feel afterward?

Use the affirmation above as often as you can. This is another great affirmation to ensure that you put somewhere that you can see it constantly throughout the day. Reminding yourself that you are capable of accomplishing anything you want to is an important part of learning how to push yourself out of your comfort zone and into a position of learning more about yourself.

The 'Comfort Zone' can be a nice place to be briefly but, it is not intended to be a permanent place of residence. When we become permanently placed in our comfort zone we tend to also become complacent and stagnant. These can be the mortal enemies of growth and development. We should always continue to try new things at least once. These things, of course, should always be harmless and potentially good for us.

There are many things that frighten us, but what is fear? Fear usually comes from a place of ignorance, not understanding something in its organic state. When we fear something we initially put a block on out mind to be open to trying to understand it. Sometimes we miss out on such beautiful experiences, opportunities, and people because of fear. Fear should be conquered and not allowed to become the conqueror. This, of course, is not very easy, there is a lot of back and forth between your decision making and your feelings. However, until you make it a point to atlas try and learn before making concrete decisions about something you are essentially allowing for the fear to overtake you and your process.

When we find that there are circumstances that make us feel scared or uncomfortable it is always a good idea to vent about it. It is not always healthy for the mind, body, or spirit to keep bad emotions inside for too long. You can choose to vent out in any way you like. Taking a wine and art session or going for a run, writing in a journal or maybe just talking it over with a close friend andTaking a wine and art session, going for a run, writing in a journal, or maybe just talking it over with a close friend or family member. When we release things that are troubling us we are lifting a burden and it feels so good!

Day Twenty-Two

Quote: "Very little is needed to make a happy life; it is all within yourself, in your way of thinking." – Marcus Aurelius

Affirmation: My life is fulfilling and makes me happy.

Some Things You Should Consider:

Realizing that living a simpler life is the most liberating movement that we can give our self is one of the best things that one can experience. It is indeed a journey as you learn that you really don't have to have everything just because it is the newest thing or the latest trend. Being yourself and eliminating the unnecessary things in your life all equals to true liberty.

Try to declutter your life and you will surely find some type of peace and serenity. There are a few things that you can try in order to obtain this:

    1. Everything that you have should have a function or hold some true sentimental value to you.

    2. Organization; everything that has a function has a space designated for itself.

    3. Take your time on things that you have to accomplish. There is no need to rush through life. When we rush through things then we are bound to make mistakes.

Finding a fulfilling life can be difficult if you don't have any way of exploration. I challenge you to go out and find something that you know absolutely nothing about and when you do, join in. You never know what will spark a new adventure in your life and what can come of it.

You are the master of your happiness. No one can determine whether you are happy except you. You make the choice regarding how you are going to react to a situation. Think about a time when you were in a negative situation, but you remained happy overall and didn't let the situation ruin your entire day or your entire week.

The quote above is one that is great for every person in the world to remember. If you can, place this quote somewhere permanent. Somewhere you are going to see it in the morning when you wake up, throughout the day and again in the evening. Telling yourself that your life is fulfilling is the first step in believing your life is fulfilling.

Success Story – Donna

"What God says you are is more important than what others think of you."

– *Lailah Gifty Akita*

My name is Donna and I must tell you, I am dead excited about affirmations. I follow the Christian faith and I always had it in my head that affirmations were nothing more than New-Age nonsense but I'm here to tell you that they are not and I have found them so incredibly useful.

Most of us watch the Olympics when it's on the TV. I watched the recent Winter Olympics because it gives me inspiration. I see people who have found true success at what they do, people who compete to be the top of their field, their game. They are incredibly focused on what they are doing and, to get to where they are, they have spent virtually every day working towards their goal, preparing themselves and taking part in all the major competitions and other events that happen along the way. They have succeeded at all these events and now they are at the Olympics, champions.

There is one thing that stands out with these athletes; before they compete in their event, they close their eyes and rehearse what they are going to do in their minds. They visualize themselves skiing down the slope, racing that course; they rehearse the routines that they have done so many times before and they feel their muscles working those movements They see it all happening and that happens because they think about it and they practice repeatedly.

I used to play the violin professionally and would practice for a minimum of 5 hours every single day, as well as taking part in rehearsals. It seemed I would always be preparing myself, practicing for a concert and I always had a deadline to work to. I had a specific goal in mind, either of being the best musician I could be or of joining a violinist group and performing with them. When I wasn't physically practicing, I would be mentally practicing.

Affirmations are the same. I asked myself some questions — "where do I want to be in 5 years?", "how healthy do I want to be?", "How successful do I want to be?" and a whole host of other similar questions. Then I asked myself what I should do NOW to get to where I wanted to be in 5 years' time. I never once said to myself that I couldn't achieve it. Instead, I told myself that to be successful, I needed to certain things, the same way that every successful person does. If a successful person got there by eating food that was raw and living and drinking only green tea, then that is what I had to do. If I wanted the same success I had to do the same things.

My next step was to come up with an action plan, a schedule that included these activities I needed to do on a daily basis. I kept saying to myself the affirmation, "Successful people do ABC and because I am a successful person, I must also do ABC". It really didn't take long for everything to fall into place!

My daily affirmations are extremely simple. I say them every morning and I say them every night before I go to bed. I also say them throughout the day as well. I am fighting a disease called muscular dystrophy so one of my daily affirmations is, "I am a very powerful and strong woman". My spirit and my mind tell me it is true and I know that the more I say this affirmation, the more my cells will understand that it is true. Already, I am able to move in ways that I couldn't do several weeks ago.

One thing I do have to be careful of is thought processes and attitude. It is very easy to get wound up in negative thinking, such as, "I am never going to be well again, I will never make a good marriage/mother/wife, I will never have plenty of money" and things like that. But, by using positive affirmations every day, and pushing the negative ones out of my life, I can truly say that my life has changed so much and all of it for the better.

I can see the changes happening in my mind and I keep an eye on the daily actions that I do to make sure I am continually moving forwards, toward my personal goals and not away from them. I write down small goals that are achievable so that I can see them in black and white. This makes me more likely to do them and I will repeat my positive affirmations, stop negative thoughts from forming and it truly works.

A positive affirmation is saying something to yourself that you deeply believe to be true or what you would like to be true; it is in effect, putting faith into action. If you read a passage in the bible that says, "I want nothing more than to see you prosper and be in health" then it is perfectly fine for your affirmation to be, "I am prosperous and healthy, by my faith."

Chapter 5: Phase Four – Days Twenty-Three Through Thirty

*"Keep your thoughts positive, because your thoughts become your words.
Keep your words positive, because your words become your behavior.
Keep your behavior positive, because your behavior becomes your habits.
Keep your habits positive, because your habits become your values.
Keep your values positive, because your values become your destiny." –
Mahatma Gandhi*

You have made it through the first three phases of this book. Let's take a minute and analyze how your thoughts have changed while you have been reading this book. Consider how much happier you are feeling. Think about your levels of optimism when you are facing a difficult situation. Analyze how easily you are conceding defeat and how much harder you are trying to meet your goals.

Another thing to consider is the challenge back from phase one. Have you still been getting up a little bit earlier in the morning to work on reading and thinking about the quotes and affirmations? Do you feel as though waking up a little bit earlier has become a routine now? Think about how you feel after reading the quotes and affirmations. Are you finding yourself looking forward to seeing what the next day has in store for you? Consider if your days are feeling more positive after reading your daily quote and affirmation.

This phase is going to be set up a little bit differently than the last three phases were. Over the last twenty-two days, I have given you both the quote and the affirmation for you to think about and apply to your life. While I am still going to give you the quote each day, this week's challenge is going to require you to come up with your affirmations that are more personal to you.

Challenge – Phase Four: Coming up with your affirmations isn't going to be difficult. By coming up with your affirmations, they are going to be more meaningful and powerful in your life and your situation. The reason they are more powerful is that they are personalized to your life and your way of thinking. When you use a personalized affirmation instead of one that is generic and not geared to your specific situation it becomes something that you own and that you know geared towards making your life better. This is going to enable you to feel more connected to the words.

You are not going to be alone in this challenge. Each day I am going to guide you through the process of creating your affirmation, working off the quotes that have been included. I am going to guide you through the creation of the affirmation to be sure that you are creating effective affirmations that are going to genuinely benefit your life. Affirmations that don't benefit you are useless. If at any time you find that a particular affirmation is no longer useful to you, switch it out with something else that is of use to you and your life.

How To Write An Effective Affirmation:

Before we move on and have you writing your affirmations, here is a quick outline of what an effective affirmation needs to contain.

- Write an affirmation that is a positive spin on a negative thought or situation. The language you are using is incredibly important. You want to write an affirmation that is going to resonate with you on a personal level.

- Write in the present tense as often as you can. While writing affirmations in the future tense can be acceptable sometimes, it makes it sound as though it is a goal you are going to reach for in the future instead of something you want to see in your life right now. When you have a goal that you are going to work towards sometime in the future, it is not an effective goal, and the same is true for affirmations.

- Avoid words that elicit judgment. Words like never and always are very strong and judgmental words. You want your affirmation to be gentle and bring relief from judgments.

- Make your affirmations personal. Use the pronouns 'I' and 'My' in your affirmations to raise the level of commitment and belief you are going to have in the affirmation.

- Remember to keep your affirmations realistic and direct.

Day Twenty-Three

Quote: "Success is not final; failure is not fatal: it is the courage to continue that counts" – Winston Churchill

Affirmation:

To create your affirmation today, think of something that you are currently working on that you feel as though you should quit. This can be something big like a job or relationship, or it could be something small like a goal to go to the gym or read a different book each month. Choose something that you feel like you aren't successful at, but you also don't want to quit. Avoid choosing something like smoking, as that isn't going to fit into this style of affirmation.

The definition of enduring is continuing or long-lasting. The definition of endurance is the fact or power of enduring an unpleasant or difficult process or situation without giving way. We all must have the will to have endurance through hard times. Without endurance there is no progression, and if there is no progression, there is no ultimate recovery.

When you face having to endure a difficult position in life there are a few ways that you can try and abide by:

- Remember that suffering is only temporary and is only as temporary or permanent as one makes it.

- Understand that you cannot fix everything all at one time and that some things are momentarily out of your control.

- Be mindful of how you allow others to influence your decisions. Not everyone has knowledgeable or good intentions on your situation. Even some close friends or families who might have gone through similar things may not be the best to gain insight from. Remember that everyone goes through and handles things differently because we are all unique. What might work for one may not work for you.

Think back over some of the affirmations that you have used over the last few weeks. Many of them had a similar theme to them but were not personal to your situation. Instead, they were generic and able to be used by many different people in different situations.

Write one that is personal to the situation you chose above.

I am going to provide you with some examples as we go through this chapter and for each one I am going to relate them to a runner who is very committed to becoming a better runner but is thinking about giving up because he hasn't successfully run five miles. An example of his affirmation could be: "I am strong enough to go to the gym. I have the stamina to run five miles."

Remember to use only positive words. Using something like "I am not too tired to go to the gym" is not going to be as effective as "I have the energy to go to the gym." Replace any negative words and thoughts with something positive and reassuring.

Day Twenty-Four

Quote: "Getting over a painful experience is much like crossing monkey bars. You have to let go at some point to move forward." – Clive S. Lewis

Affirmation:

We have all gone through painful experiences in our lifetime. Sometimes we can let them go and move on and other times we hold onto those things and let them determine where our lives are going.

Think about something you failed at that you haven't tried to do again because you failed. This can be as big or small as you would like it to be. Remember, starting with something that is small and insignificant isn't going to produce the same results as starting with something meaningful.

Here is an example using the runner I used yesterday. Let's say our runner went to the gym and practiced every day and signed up for a five-mile marathon, but after four miles broke his ankle in three places and needed a lot of rehabilitation before he could even attempt to walk again, never mind run. He could give up on running, which would be easy. Or, he could use an affirmation like this: "My body is strong. I will begin running again."

Using an affirmation like this is going to out the runner into the mindset not to give up and to let go of the fall he had and keep focusing on moving forwards.

Just like yesterday, keep the affirmation positive and don't use any words that have a negative connotation. Negative words tend to stick in your brain as negative words, even if used in a positive way.

When we go through a painful event in our lives we can use that circumstance to help discover or re-discover who we are. There are so many instances where we can learn from reflecting on a loss, traumatic experience or an accident from the past. Although going through the healing process can be a very hard and painful time but it is necessary if you are going to grow. Through that process, we often find the chance to gain self-discovery and resolution.

What are some things you have learned and or gained from a painful event in your life? How has this changed the way that you view life? Have you found any closure or is this painfulness still in control of your everyday life?

We must all go through the process of gaining closure. Closure is absolutely necessary when desiring to move on from a certain situation. These situations don't necessarily have to be negative but the majority of people are seeking closure from hurtful events in their lives. Just like a physical scar we can carry emotional scars and like any type of physical wound, it takes time to heal. So it is from an emotional wound.

When you have reached closure of something you have made peace and understanding with it. You know that it happened, recognized that it took place, understand that it cannot be changed and that it is what it is. Acceptance of what has taken place and the drive to move forward is all a part of what true closure is. There isn't an easy way to find closure, just like a snowflake, everyone's approach to gaining closure is different from the next ones. After acceptance then comes the of origin of healing and eventually being able to move forward.

Day Twenty-Five

Quote: "Life's most persistent and urgent question is, 'what are you doing for others?" – Martin Luther King, Jr.

Affirmation:

A couple of phases ago, your challenge was to spread happiness to at least one person every day. Were you successful in that challenge? Did you continue going out of your way to make people happy as the days progressed? Today's affirmation is going to be about what you do for the people around you on a regular basis. Consider how much you donate. Whether it is donating your time volunteering, your money or your old belongings, do you believe you are doing everything you can do to help other people?

We are going to use the same runner that we have been using previously for our examples. We know that he is a good runner, and now he wants to help people out with his skills. His affirmation may look something like this: "I can raise awareness of safety while running." Or "I am going to talk to people about overcoming obstacles and not giving up on themselves." This demonstrates that the runner is using his experiences to educate others.

Think about things you can do that would help someone else. It's okay to go out of your way for another person. This affirmation doesn't need to be as specific as "I am going to help Susie with her homework." It can be something like "I am going to donate my time to [a cause that is important to you)" Remember, don't just say it. Act on your affirmation as well. Following through on your affirmation is just as important as creating your affirmation.

There is a great beauty behind helping others. You are creating something meaningful in another person's life. There's no rule to being kind other that you doing something out of pure dedication and from a place of love. Doing something without seeking anything in return is my definition of kindness. There is a difference in having providing a service for someone 'just because' and providing a service for someone to gain validity. When we seek validation from something that was supposed to be done from the heart we are opening up ourselves to disappointment. The disappointment comes from when we are expecting to get rewarded for being kind and then it never comes.

One of the biggest secrets to being happy is by giving to others. Being charitable. Being proactive for a great cause. You don't have to know or be personally close with an individual to give the never ending gift of kindness.

For those who are wondering "Why should I give to others?'" there are many reasons:

- You can begin to fill that emptiness you may have and gain a feeling of meaningfulness for yourself as well as others.

- Serving other people can create a domino effect that never seems to end.

- Helping others can help you grow into a person with strong leadership skills.

If you are not sure where to start being kind here are a few suggestions:

-Volunteer! Volunteer! Volunteer! There are so many groups and organizations that host several opportunities to give to the local communities that you are surrounded by. This is a great way to begin understanding how to give without expecting anything in return. You can gain valuable life experiences and skills. Learn something new about yourself and the cause that you are volunteering for. Most importantly you are doing something for the good of someone or something else.

- Donation. This is a wonderful way to show kindness. That t-shirt that's sitting around collecting dust, or that old set of dinnerware that's in the attic are examples of things that can be given to a person or family that is in true need. There are even community activism groups that take donations from anonymous givers if you are a little on the shy side.

-Share some kind words. If you like someone's hairstyle or their smile, tell them. Our words and the way that we use them have such an impact on the people around us and also ourselves.

-Homemade Gifts! If you are artistically inclined then I employ you to get creative and make something by hand. There are so many people who greatly appreciate the fact of someone taking time to actually make something to show appreciation and kindness for that individual. A candle, a wreath, a photo album, or maybe even some baked goods are all wonderful ideas of things to make for someone else.

<u>Remember</u>: It is always better to give than to receive.

Day Twenty-Six

Quote: "Do not dwell in the past, do not dream of the future, concentrate the mind on the present moment" – Buddha

Affirmation:

Do you know what it means to be mindful? Being mindful means that you are present in each moment. Living in the now. The quote above sums it up completely, —avoid dwelling on the past and the future and focus on the present moment that you are living. Notice all the small things that are happening around. Don't get so caught up in thinking about how your day at work was, or the project that you have due tomorrow that you miss all the little things going on at this moment.

Think about your personal life. Where do your thoughts tend to dwell? Consider if you are constantly stuck in the past or if you are more concerned about where your future is going to bring you. Does this action result in you becoming withdrawn or dislocated from your relationships and interactions with others?

Our runner is focused on running in the next marathon. Because of this focus, he tends to forget his commitments to his family, and this creates a lot of tension. Some of his affirmations may include:

- "I have the focus to be present in the moment."
- "The future will take care of itself. My family is more important than running."
- "I can be present in the moment and be a good runner."

Think about people who are close to you that may feel as though you are always distracted. If this affirmation is harder to write up, consider asking those who are closest to you if they feel like you give them your undivided attention. In personal relationships, this is very important. If your loved ones feel like you are constantly unavailable and inattentive, even when you are physically present, then that can become a serious problem within the relationship that needs to be resolved as soon as possible. When we hurt the ones who truly love us we are not only damaging them but we are in all actuality hurting ourselves as well. Many of us are fortunate to have at least one supporter, if not many in our lives and we should take care not to tarnish that relationship. They can turn out to be one of our greatest inspirations in achieving a goal.

Day Twenty-Seven

Quote: "In the long run the pessimist may be proved right, but the optimist has a better time on the trip." – Daniel L. Reardon

Affirmation:

We have spent a lot of time analyzing optimism and pessimism, and you should be able to identify which of the two categories you fall into. We have also looked at a couple of different quotes about enjoying the moment instead of focusing on only where we want to go. While that is the focus of this quote, I want you to take your affirmation in a slightly different direction.

Last week your challenge was to make a list of negative situations and something positive that came out of it. Today you are going to come up with three things about yourself that you don't like, and you are going to spin them into positive affirmations.

For example; Our runner suffers from insomnia, he feels that he is always snapping at his children, and he never makes time for his wife. His affirmations would look like this:

- "I am completely free from insomnia," While this isn't yet true, by telling himself repeatedly that it is true, he is going to bring the relief from insomnia into his life.

- "It is deeply satisfying for me to respond with wisdom, love, firmness, and self-control when my children misbehave," By reminding himself how he should respond to his children, he is more likely to respond the way he wants to.

- "It is important to me to spend time with my wife daily. I love my wife and want to see her happy." Using this affirmation is going to make his wife more important to our runner and is going to make spending time with her a priority.

Remember: We are what we think.

Come up with three or more affirmations for yourself that are specific to things about you or your life that you are unhappy with. Try to make these three affirmations ones that you would want to be saying every day.

Day Twenty-Eight

Quote: "To change your life, you have to change yourself. To change yourself you have to change your mindset." – Wilson Kanadi

Affirmation:

We all know that change is not an easy thing to accept, especially once we have been conditioned into a normalcy. Change can often be frightening, positive, slow, gainful, disciplinary, and repetitive. Changing your mindset is not an easy thing to do, but if you want to see some real changes in your life, you need to change how you are looking at things. Our view on situations and how we handle them are mirrored reflection of how our thought processes operate. Many people have many different ways on how to go about facing a situation or changing a problem. Though the flexibility of the multiple ways you can attempt to rectify a situation on you know what will and won't work for you. As we are coming to the end of our thirty days together, it is vital that you can keep up the changes that you have begun making. That is the purpose behind today's affirmation.

To create today's affirmation, you are going to consider what your biggest obstacles in doing the challenges in this book have been. Perhaps you have struggled with making time each day to sit and read and think about the quote and affirmation. Maybe you found that you had a hard time saying the affirmations out loud and believing in them. Or, perhaps it was acknowledging your flaws that you have the hardest time with. Whatever it was that you had a hard time with, use all the knowledge you have about affirmations to create an affirmation to counter whatever your biggest struggle may be.

When we begin to evolve trough the act of change it must be protected. A new way of doing things are as fragile as making a soufflé and can fall through the cracks if precaution of management isn't taken into account. One way to do this is to have control of what surrounds you. What goes on in your environment plays a huge role in how you respond to stimuli. It helps to keep a note of what triggers in your environment, both good and bad, play a role in how you are changing. If you find that there are some things that are hindering your growth then you should find new tactics on how to dismiss it from your life. However, if there are good things that help you when changing these things should be increased in any way possible.

Remember that change is a process. A process that usually takes some time, although there is no logically acclaimed amount of time that it takes to reach the conclusion of that journey called change, it is safe to say that it does not always happen overnight. It's okay to divide goals and aspirations into smaller missions. Be patient with yourself and don't rush. This helps you to keep track of how far you have come and how much more you have to go. It allows you to notice the good and the bad of what has had to happen to allow you to reach your milestone. When you focus on these small successes this builds so much great self-esteem and drive that will keep you moving forward.

Don't forget to reward yourself on reaching these small goals. Treat yourself! Remember that you are what's important here and when you achieve a goal it's perfectly okay to reward yourself with something good, healthy, and beneficial. A trip to the spa, or a night out with the fellas to celebrate, a slice of cake from your favorite bakery, or that new outfit you've had your eye on. These treats can help keep you motivated as you continue to change.

Day Twenty-Nine

Quote: "Most of the important things in the world have been accomplished by people who had kept on trying when there seemed no hope at all." – Dale Carnegie

Affirmation:

Sometimes we hit a point in our lives where things seem hopeless. Chances are, you have been there before, and you will experience that again. Today we are going to create an affirmation for a time when things are feeling hopeless. Even if you aren't in a hopeless situation right now, it is important to have an affirmation that is going to allow you to boost yourself up. This is both to avoid a hopeless situation and to help you out of it if you find yourself in a hopeless situation.

When we begin to feel hopeless in a situation this can affect our day to day activities. We can begin to show the onset signs of depression, isolation, avoidance and not being engaging with others. When you are feeling hopeless you question yourself if something is really worth it or if it is just a waste of time. This is the moment when you must remember that "we are what we think," when you think negatively then you are directing that type of energy into your situation.

When confronting the feeling of hopelessness the number one thing I can think of doing first is trying something new. The beauty of trying something new is it is in a foreign world. Trying something new encourages us to be courageous, open-minded, adventurous, and inquisitive. These are all wonderful attributes to have going through life. You never know where your next inspiration may come from so it's important to venture out and try new things when you have feelings of hopelessness.

Think about a time when you have felt hopeless in the past. What is something someone said to you that helped you, or something you wish someone had said to you?

We are going to go back to our runner to demonstrate an example. Our runner is getting ready to run an eight-mile marathon. The marathon states that the eight miles must be completed in forty minutes to earn a medal. Our runner desperately wants this medal, but the best time he can get is fifty minutes, and he feels hopeless. Here are a couple of affirmations he could use:

- "I can run eight miles in forty minutes."

- "I am a successful runner; I have earned my times."
- "My family loves me, and I am a great person just the way I am."

As you can see, the third example is a little more generic than the first two. While you want to be as specific as possible, sometimes an affirmation that leans towards being generic is helpful as you can apply it to more aspects of your life. If this is an affirmation you are going to keep in your reserves for when you need it, a generic affirmation can be altered to match a situation later, when the situation presents itself.

Day Thirty

Quote: "Why Worry? If you've done the very best you can, worrying won't make it any better" – Walt Disney

Affirmation:

Knowing that you have done the best you can in any situation is an important part of being at peace with the decisions you have made and the outcomes of those decisions. As we end this book, you may be worried about moving into using affirmations on your own. Don't be. By doing the best you could throughout this book, you have undergone a transformation in your thinking, and you are now ready to move forward on your own.

Worrying can have a direct effect on our physical health; causing headaches, gastrointestinal complications, anxiety, sleep disruptions, hormone imbalances, and much more...

When facing worry we have to realize that it is an emotion and an emotion that is defined as a natural instinctive state of mind which comes from a person's circumstances. In other words, it's totally natural to worry about something at one point or another. However, when you allow this worry to take over your life you are opening yourself to potentially becoming dysfunctional and in a monotonous routine.

Worrying about what is going to happen next is something that we are all guilty of, but doesn't accomplish anything. Instead of requiring you to create your affirmation today, I am going to give you five affirmations that are about not worrying. I want you to read through them and choose the one that you feel is the most natural for you to say. Take this affirmation and change the words to make it personal and about you.

- "I am letting go of my worries."
- "I am able to solve problems and worries using logic."
- "I will be relaxed and calm."
- "I am a naturally calm person."
- "I am confident and at peace with my life right now."

Success Story – Karen

"If you are determined to achieve your dreams, you must be ready to accept and affirm positive things about yourself. Affirm positively! Say positive things and encourage yourself that you can make it." – Israelmore Ayivor

My name is Karen and I want to tell you about my personal experience with affirmations. Recently, I learned a great deal about using affirmations to lose weight, about how it worked and now I want to share my experiences with you.

My whole life has been about one big search. I always had it in my mind that there was something terribly important that we had all forgotten, something about living how we do on earth and I have always believed that we the human race, are far powerful than we ever knew.

One way or another, I have been on this diet or that one ever since I was a teenager. I am now in my middle fifties. When I diet these days, no matter what I do, no matter how much I restrict what I eat, nothing happens. I can, however, put weight on easily when I eat normally.

I decided that I needed to change the way I was thinking, to start thinking positive things about losing weight. What else did I have to lose? Diets weren't working anymore so the very first thing I thought was that I was never going to go on another diet again. And it is to this that I attribute the success of my affirmations. When you think about it, the act of dieting causes a feeling of lacking. I firmly believe that your unconsciousness believes that you are starving when you go on a diet and, as such, it holds on fast to all that stored fat so that, when you "starve" yourself again, it can feed you and keep you alive. It is also this very thing that causes you to gain every single pound of fat back; it has absolutely no consideration of the good or the bad about losing weight.

Recently, I put on weight, about 8 lbs. so I changed my affirmation. I said to myself, *"I am …. lbs."*. I made it 8 lbs. lower than what I weighed and I said it every single night before I went to bed, as well as every single morning when I got up. However, it was also a mantra that I repeated through the course of the day and during the night if I woke. Two weeks later, I weighed myself; nothing had changed. After three weeks, those 8 lbs. had disappeared.

When I tried this gain, I lowered my affirmation weight by 10 lbs. and kept repeating my affirmation every day for two months. Nothing happened so I thought it must have been a fluke the first time around. I tried again but this time reducing my weight but just 5 lbs. It did work but it took a month. I tried again with the 5 lbs. reduction but this time, I could repeat the affirmation much more than I could before and it only took two weeks to work this time.

This month, I am concentrating on other things but I will return to my weight loss soon. What is interesting this time is that, no matter what I eat, I have neither gained any weight nor lost it? My unconscious is under the belief that I will weight whatever my last affirmation was, no matter what I do, or until I tell it otherwise.

I hope this will encourage you to give affirmations a try. You do need to be able to stick to it and push on even though you may want to give but it will work; it did for me where nothing else would.

Chapter 6: What if it Doesn't Work?

Muhammad Ali had one affirmation that he used to use repeatedly until he became the words he spoke – *"I AM THE GREATEST"*

Provided they are used properly, affirmations have been scientifically proven to be a truly effective means of becoming who you want to be, the person you must become to achieve all that you want to achieve throughout life. However, affirmations have also been given something of a bad time because many people have tried them and have failed to achieve what they want.

The reason they have failed is because things have changed. For many decades, so-called gurus and experts told us that we should be doing affirmations in a specific way, a way that is destined to be completely ineffective and will only cause failure, no matter how much you try them. There are two problems here:

First off, if you lie to yourself, it simply won't work. Saying things like:

"I am a millionaire" when you clearly aren't

"My body fat is only 7%" when it most certainly isn't

"I have achieved every goal I set for myself in the last year" when you really haven't

All of this is going to fail because you are lying to yourself. This way of saying affirmations, as if you have already achieved something or become something you aren't is the biggest single reason for failure. If you use this technique, every time you speak an affirmation that isn't based firmly in truth, your unconscious will kick it aside because it knows it isn't true. You are an intelligent person and repeatedly lying to yourself will never work simply because the truth will always come out.

Let's take an affirmation like, *"I am a magnet for money; money comes to me in vast amounts without any effort"*; this might make you feel fantastic while you are saying it because it takes away from your very real worries about finances but it will never ever result in income. Anyone who sits and waits for money to come to them without doing anything to make it happen will always be cash poor.

If you want to generate money in abundance, or anything else that you desire, you do have to do something to make it happen. Every action you take must be aligned with the results that you want to achieve and affirmations must both state and affirm both parts of that.

The following are four steps that will help you to create affirmations that you can implement, affirmations that will go into your conscious mind and your subconscious to produce the results that you want for success beyond what you thought possible before.

Each affirmation must be created in this way:

Step 1 – The Result That You Are Committed to Achieving and Why

Note that you are not beginning with something that you WANT. We all want something but we don't always get what we want. Instead, we only get what we are committed to achieving. So you want to be a millionaire; don't we all so come and join this club that is not exclusive. Oh, hold on, you are committed to becoming a millionaire, 100% committed and you will do whatever is necessary, the actions that you need to take to achieve that result. Now, we're on the right track.

Action - write down one very specific and extraordinary result that you are committed to achieving. Choose one that is going to challenge you and will make significant improvements to your life; improvements that you are 100% ready to commit to making. It doesn't matter yet that you don't know how you will achieve this, that will come later. Next, your affirmation must contain a reason why you are going to do this, compelling reasons and the benefit that you will get from it.

Examples

Here are some examples of affirmations written in this way:

"I am committed to increasing my income in the next year from $... to $... so that I can give my family financial security."

"I am committed 100% to losing ...lbs. and weighing ...lbs. by (input a specific date) so that I can set the right example for my children/decrease my risks of serious disease."

Step 2 – The Actions You Commit to Taking and When

It would be easy to write down an affirmation that merely says what you want without saying what you are going to do but this would be as good as pointless. In fact, it could be seen as being counter-productive because all you are doing is telling your subconscious that you can achieve the result without doing anything.

Action – Clarify exactly what you are going to do to achieve the result you want, be it an activity, an action or a habit that needs to be changed if you are going to be successful. State clearly when you will do this and how often you must do to achieve the necessary action.

Examples:

"To ensure that I increase my income, I am 100% committed to making 40 prospecting calls every day, between 8 am and 10 am, no matter what happens.

"To make sure I lose ...lbs., I am committed 100% to attending the gym every day and running for at least 20 minutes a day on the treadmill between 6 am and 7 am".

If you make your actions specific, the better they will be. Make sure that you include how often, how many and specific time frames.

Step 3 – Repeat Your Affirmation Each Morning with Emotion

Remember this; these affirmations are designed purely to make you feel better. These are statements that you have written, statements that have been engineered to program your mindset and beliefs into your subconscious so that you can achieve the outcome you want. At the same time, they will be telling your conscious mind that you need to remain focused on high priorities and carry out the actions that are going to get you to the end of your journey.

That said, if your affirmations are going to be effective, you must use emotion when you are saying them. If you repeat your affirmation over and over without feeling the truth of it, it won't work or at best, you will only get mediocre results. It is your responsibility to generate real excitement and real determination and then bring those emotions into each of your affirmations, every time you say them.

Action – Set a specific time every morning to say your affirmations. The reason for this is because you have to both program the subconscious and train the conscious mind on what is truly important to you and what your commitments are to making it happen. To do this, you must be consistent and so you have to say your affirmations at the same time every single day. Once you make these a solid part of your routine, only then will you see the results start to happen.

Step 4 – Update Your Affirmations and Evolve Them Constantly

As your commitments begin to be realized, you will improve and evolve and, because of that, your affirmations must do the same. Once you reach a goal, set up a new one and add it to your affirmation. You can have an affirmation for every part of your life that is significant – your health, finances, family, relationships, etc. – and you should evolve your affirmations on a constant basis as your learning increases.

In the next few chapters, I am going to give you some positive affirmations to say for three different areas of your life – success, health, and career, followed by some motivational ones and then I will be showing you some techniques on learning how to write and use your own affirmations. Once you have completed the 30-day course, don't stop. Continue to make these affirmations a part of your daily routine. Pick any of these affirmations or write your own and continue reaping the success that you have already experienced.

Chapter 7: Positive Affirmations for Success

Breathe in deeply a couple of times and clear out your mind – you do not need any distractions at this point. When you read these affirmations, read them with true meaning and really feel the meaning of each one deep inside of you. Repeat each one as many times as necessary until you really feel it, in your bones and in your heart.

Smile widely and make it a genuine smile and then read each of them aloud. If you need help in truly feeling the power of each one, don't be afraid to jump up and down, grab at the air and use your fists to pull that energy into you. Repeat them with real deep meaning to bring much faster results. This is the trick with affirmations – you must mean them and you have to feel them.

I am always present and I am always in the moment.

I am open to receiving great quantities wealth, health, and happiness.

My life is mine to create.

I enjoy my life. It is full of beauty and abundance.

I attract everything I need to be happy, whole and healthy and I do it effortlessly.

I am consistently finding new opportunities and successes.

I live my life wholeheartedly and with passion.

My world is filled with love, beauty, happiness, and abundance.

I deserve prosperity and abundance.

I use my unique talents and gifts to manifest abundance.

I live a life full of joy and honesty.

I deserve to live a full and complete life.

I produce financial affluence by doing what I love and loving what I do.

I am surrounded by people who love me and give me support.

People recognize my existence and they appreciate it.

My love and pure zest for life motivate and inspire other people.

I share my gifts with other people generously and I accept their gifts with genuine gratitude.

I am known for my full-of-life attitude and the positive energy I give off.

I seek mentorship and inspiration from successful people that I admire.

I listen with patience, understanding, and compassion to other people.

I communicate professionally, gracefully and clearly.

My success is vital.

I contribute an influential and positive presence to the world.

I celebrate life and the beauty of it every single day.

I live a full life.

I create the lifestyle I want to live with enthusiasm.

I choose success, happiness, and health.

I celebrate love, health, and life itself every day.

The miracle and magic of life surround me wherever I go!

Right now, every dream I have is coming true!

And so it is.

Chapter 8: Positive Affirmations for Good Health

When you are healthy you are wealthy and positive affirmations play a huge part in this. When your mind is centered around thoughts of health, your body will follow and will be healthier. We know that there is a connection between the mind and the body and it has been agreed that some diseases are psychosomatic – caused by emotion and thought.

Even those diseases that are caused by a germ can be thought of in some way as being psychosomatic because we "allow" the germs to enter our bodies or germs that already exist there will become stronger, strong enough to cause a disease simply because your immune system is not working effectively because of emotion.

All emotion is controlled completely by thought and we all know that thought can be formed entirely at will. Positive affirmations will help to mold those thoughts and that is where the connection between these affirmations and your health become clearer.

There is an old saying, *"Change Your Thoughts, Change Your Life"* and it is perfectly possible to fill up your mind with thoughts of health just by using the right positive affirmations. Repeating them over and over again will train your subconscious mind to the extent where it begins to transform your body in line with your thoughts.

Believe it or now, and I would never make light of a subject like this, there have been cases of cancer being overcome by the power of thought. You all know about placebos and it is well known that in medical terms, the placebo effect is psychological, i.e. in your mind. A patient would be given a sugar pill instead of the real medication but would be told that it was the real thing needed to cure his condition. And in many cases, it will cure it because the patient is convinced he is taking the proper medication the placebo itself does nothing; it is all in his mind. Affirmations can have the same effect on your body.

There is also evidence that different mental emotions cause different chemicals to be produced in your body. When you are feeling happy, the chemicals produced are beneficial to your body. When you are feeling sad, those chemicals are harmful to your body. As such, your thoughts affect what your body feels and does. It is very clear that positive affirmations can have very positive health effects on your body.

Below is a list of health affirmations. Choose only those that fit your situation and repeat 100 times every day for a period of 6 months. If you are on any medication that has been prescribed for your condition, DO NOT, under any circumstances, stop taking it. Affirmations are designed as a way of complementing the medication, not replacing it, and they will help to strengthen your mind, change your thought direction and assist your body in healing.

Every single day, in every single way, I am getting better and healthier

I love myself and I am healthy

Every single cell throughout my body is conscious of health. I am a health nut

My mind is perfectly calm and full of peace and my body is full of vitality and energy

I don't eat junk; I eat nutritious healthy food that is beneficial to my body and I drink large quantities of water to cleanse my system

I only think positive thoughts and I am always joyful and happy, no matter what life throws at me

I always feel great and my body feels great; I radiate positivity and happiness

Every single day is a brand-new day of health, happiness, and hope

It is my birthright to be healthy. I take good care of my body and I bless it daily

I am always happy, hearty and hale. Happy in spirit, hearty in disposition and hale in body

My heart is strong and my body is steel. I am full of energy, vitality and am vigorous

Godliness is first, good health is second. I possess a healthy body and a healthy mind

With each day that passes, my body becomes healthier and full of energy

My body is a temple. It is clean, holy and good

I practice deep breathing, take regular exercise and only eat healthy nutritious foods

I am free of high/low blood pressure, I am free of diabetes and am free of any other disease that may threaten my life

I release any ill feelings I have, about anything or anyone and I forgive everyone that is associated with me

Every day, I thank God and I thank everybody in my life. I know that, without you all, I am not a complete person and I thank you for coming into and for staying in my life

My Motto is "Healthy, wealthy and wise". I have a healthy body, I have wealth and I have a wise mind

I am my creator. I am the one, I am the All

Chapter 9: Positive Affirmations for your Career

The positive career affirmations I am going to tell you will help you to see your goals, your career, your attitude and your relationships with everyone you work with or for more clearly. The definition of a career is, "a chosen pursuit, a profession or an occupation; the general course or progression of one's working life or one's professional achievements".

It is perfectly natural to want a successful career in the job or area that you choose and we all want to do a good job, to enjoy it and to earn enough money. You can choose a career in a specific job, in a specific profession or a business and it is perfectly possible to earn job satisfaction and a good reward in financial terms in any of these three areas, provided you are prepared to take the right steps necessary to ensure it.

There are lots of important things, not least knowledge in your chosen field, hard work, and proper planning, not to mention a real vision. However, more important is having the right attitude mentally. Thomas Jefferson once said, *nothing can stop the man with the right mental attitude from achieving his goal; nothing on earth can help the man with the wrong mental attitude."*

At times, we all need a good boost mentally in our work; we sometimes need to give ourselves a good talking to and this is where positive career affirmations can help you immensely. The affirmations I have listed below are going to help you get in tune with the work you do, in turn with your colleagues, your bosses, and your juniors. They will help you to get your priorities in the right order and help to focus your mind on your career.

Pick one or more from this list. You can use them on their own or you can combine them to make your own affirmations that suit your circumstances. Repeat your affirmations 100 times a day as a minimum, standing in front of a mirror as you say them. Over time, your mindset will change and you will become more successful in your career.

At this moment, I am working in the job of my dreams

I love my career; I get total job satisfaction from it

I love my career; It lets me grow and gives me good financial reward

I can balance my family and my career so that they work together

I am valued at my place of work and I am always listened to respectfully

I have a good relationship with my boss and all my colleagues

I am content because the work I do doesn't just benefit me; it also benefits the society that I live in

My job has fantastic career prospects, opportunities for promotion and great financial compensation

Because I have such a positive attitude mentally, I always get the best projects and the best people to help me with them

I am always full of enthusiasm and this rubs off on my colleagues, resulting in a fantastic and productive working day for everyone

I was born to be an entrepreneur. Whenever opportunities arise, I recognize then and I seize them

I am a master at sales. My customers trust me and they love me and my order book is always full to overflowing

I have a work ethic that makes sure I always get the pay raises and the promotions

My forte is my self-discipline. In my home, my family comes first and in my workplace, work comes first

I always take responsibility for my work and my actions. My work motto is, "The buck stops here".

I practice diligence in my work, honesty in my attitude and have a positive mindset at all times which opens up new opportunities for me

I look after my junior staff and I help them in the appropriate way. I am friendly toward my colleagues and show respect to my seniors

To me, a career is just the means to the end. The end is the total fulfillment of my true potential and happiness and my career gives me that every day.

I do my very best in my career every single day and I give everything with no reservations. The fruits of that labor taste very sweet

My one aim is to satisfy my customers and I always give everything to be the best that I can be and to achieve that aim

Chapter 10: Positive Affirmations for Motivation

No matter what you do in life, the most important thing is motivation. Positive motivational affirmations will give you the strength that you need to start any task and see it right through to completion. It is the motivation that allows you start that task or start any action that is needed to help you reach your goal. Without that motivation, you may start out with all the best intentions but they will soon wither away and you will give up or only do a half-hearted job.

Think of motivation as the protein that builds up the muscles and as the carbohydrate that fuels you with the energy you need to complete the task that takes you to your goal. Positive affirmations are fuel; the feed the actions and, while you can start a job or a task without any motivation, you need it to finish Repeating these affirmations regularly will provide you with an inner sense of motivation, an urge to get on and do what must be done without any pushing and prompting, from you or from others. Your actions will be on a kind of auto-pilot until your goal is reached.

There is evidence from studies that finds we radiate those thoughts that are in our minds the most often. In turn, those thoughts will attract to you the circumstances that favor those thoughts and favor the people around you who have similar thoughts. Throughout this book, I have given you several quotes – don't underestimate the importance of these. They are an important resource for motivation because they tend to contain pearls of wisdom from people who are successful, whose words come from their life experiences. That makes them invaluable because there is no better teacher than life itself.

Like every other type of affirmation, a motivational affirmation is simple to prepare. Simply think about the task you are going to do and take note of the positive thoughts that enter your mind. Formulate those thoughts and include them in your affirmations, like the following examples:

I can! I can do it! I can!

When I have clear intentions, the universe will cooperate with me and I can do anything

I think only positive thoughts and only positive things are happening in my life

I am one of life's go-getters and I will do anything to achieve my goals

Success is my middle name. I am successful at everything I do

The doors that lead to opportunity are always open and I take full advantage of them with no exception

Motivation comes easily and quickly to me and I can motivate others

I am filled with hope and with energy and I live my life fully

I love challenges and I face them head on and win

Motivation is inside of me; I motivate myself

My only option in life is success. I push forward and I succeed

I make a difference to other people and I try to help them to the best of my ability

My ultimate goal is motivation. I only see the goal until I get to it

I know what my worth is and I know that I deserve success; I get success

My work is a true motivator and I will not stop until I achieve my goal

I love life; it is fulfilling and it is beautiful

Chapter 11: Preparing and Using Your Own Affirmations

So, you now know that, if you want to change your beliefs and make a new reality for yourself, you must constantly bombard your mind, conscious and subconscious, with the thoughts of what you truly desire. However, it is very important that you word these thoughts carefully otherwise, you may not get the results that you are looking for. As such, there are several things that you must do, or not do as the case may be, to get the best result out of your affirmations. I already mentioned some of these earlier but, as with affirmations, it doesn't hurt to repeat things!

- Always do your affirmations in the present tense. The past is gone and cannot be changed. Using the future tense simply tells your mind that you will do something in the future, not that you are doing it now.

Your subconscious mind will always try, very literally, to do what is asked of it. As such, you should say things like, "I am rich", "I have wealth beyond belief", I am ready to be rich and to prosper", or "II choose to be prosperous"

Psychologists say that using the term "choose" is far better because then it becomes your choice. Bear in mind one thing that is very true – what your life is now is because of choices that you have made in the past

- Always be positive because only a positive affirmation will truly work

The subconscious mind struggles to deal with negatives so if you were to say something like, "I am not overweight", by the time it reaches your subconscious, the word "not" has been removed or is ignored and that statement turns into "I am overweight".

What really happens comes down to a law we call "Focus and Growth". By this law, whatever you truly focus on will grow. So, when you say to yourself, "I am not overweight", the focus is firmly on "overweight". Your subconscious mind concentrates all its efforts on keeping you or making you overweight so it is far better to say something like, "I am slim and fit" or, "I weigh … kgs/lbs.".

- Positive affirmations can be written down or they can be spoken

When you speak your positive affirmations out loud, say them emphatically, throughout the course of the day. At the very least, what you should be doing is saying each one twenty times every morning, when you get up and then twenty times before you go to bed. This will fix that affirmation into your mind. Even better, say them 100 times a day. The more you can repeat them, the better the result will be.

If you choose to write your affirmations, write each one down at least fifteen times a day. Writing is the fastest way to impress something into your subconscious mind. Have you ever heard of Scott Adams? He is a world-famous cartoonist, known for "Dilbert" and he is the perfect example of how important written affirmations are. Go find some "Dilbert" and you will see exactly what I mean. Then we have the Mirror technique, which I will tell you more about in a short while.

- Repetition is vital.

If you really want your life to change significantly in any way, your affirmations must be repeated through the day. In time, the more you repeat them, they will become a reality to you and not just words. If you were to do them for just a few days, you shouldn't expect to see the results that you want. You must be like a dog with a bone; keep on going at them until you have achieved your goals.

There is an old story that demonstrates this:

There are two villages, side by side, A and B. Both villages always suffered from a shortage of water. The village called A suddenly discovered a rain dance that they performed and it rained. When they saw this, the village called B also did this rain dance but they never got any rain. They did it a few times, still, no rain fell. In the end, the chief of B went to see the chief of A to ask him for some help. The chief of A simply said to him, "we do this dance until the rains come; we don't do the dance and stop, expecting it to happen"

The same applies to your affirmations – do them and do them continually until you get the result you desire.

The Mirror Technique

One of the best methods for doing positive affirmations is the Mirror Technique and it has been used by many of the greatest authors of self-help books. Here is how to do it:

Stand before your mirror and look deeply into your own eyes. Repeat your affirmations with total gusto and enthusiasm. Fill them with energy. When you look into your own eyes, you will find it much easier to make the connection with your subconscious mind

You must do this regularly. In fact, whenever you are in your own home and you walk past a mirror of any description, stop, consider it, into your eyes and repeat those affirmations several times. This is an incredibly powerful technique and I guarantee you that, done regularly, it will work

The Card Technique

This is another well-known technique and here's how it's done:

Take a piece of card, 3" by 5", or a size that fits into your wallet or your pocket. On it, write your chosen affirmation in large bold lettering. Look at this card frequently throughout the day. It doesn't matter where you are; you can easily whip the card out, read it and then put it back. Don't show it to anyone and don't tell anyone what you are doing because sharing it with others will eliminate all the energy that you have put into the affirmation. Do try and look at the card at least ten times a day, if not more. The more you do it, the more chance there is of your subconscious mind getting to work quicker and bringing about your desires.

Affirmations have been of huge help to thousands upon thousands of people across the world, helping to bring about significant changes, changes that they truly want to happen. But they don't seem to work for everyone so, how can these powerful things bring success for one but fail completely for another?

Affirmations will work to program your subconscious into believing what you are stating. The simple reason for this is, your mind has no idea of the difference between reality and fantasy. When you watch a movie, for example, and you laugh at something or you cry, your mind is displaying empathy with the situation and the characters on the screen, even though it isn't real.

There are two types of affirmation – positive and negative. Most of us can, no doubt, go back to our childhoods and can remember being told that we couldn't do something, we didn't have the ability necessary, whether we were told it by a parent, a teacher, even a coach or a friend. They might have told you that were clumsy or fat. These statements stay with you for life. They hide either in your subconscious or conscious mind, and they will be reinforced throughout your entire life – unless you do something to stop them.

According to the Grandfather of Psychology of the Self, Heinz Kohut, fear of failing is more often than not connected to a fear we had in childhood of being abandoned, be it emotionally or physically. When you are afraid of failure, you will automatically overestimate the risks that you are taking and you will always come up with the absolute worst-case scenario. This is the emotional twin of the fear of being abandoned. You will go out of your way to avoid any opportunities that could lead to success and, when you fail, which is inevitable in this case, you are simply reaffirming that negative affirmation, be it something like, "Success will never come to me" or "Success just isn't meant to be in my life".

If that belief has been rooted deeply into your subconscious, it will almost certainly walk all over any positive affirmations, even if you are not aware of it. Therefore positive affirmations don't always work for everyone – their thought patterns have been strongly afflicted by something negative and this is so strong that it can knock away any positives. That said, you can get over this. There are ways to add strength to a positive affirmation so that it can win over the negative. Here we look at a few suggestions on how to make positive affirmations truly work for you:

5 Steps to Making Positive Affirmations More Powerful and Effective
Step 1

Write down in a list everything that you have always considered to be a negative quality of yours. Make sure that you include criticisms that others have made about you, anything that you may have been holding on to. It doesn't matter what it is – it could be something a friend has said to you recently, something your parents, a teacher or a sibling said to you in your childhood or what your boss said to you in your last performance review.

Make sure that you do not, at this stage, judge whether these statements are accurate and do keep in mind that every single person has flaws, whether they believe it or not.

This is one of the simple beauties of being a human being – just write everything down and then look for common threads. It could be something like, "I'm not worthy". This is a great place to begin making changes in your life, positive changes.

When you write down that belief, the one that recurs throughout your statements, take note of whether you are hanging on to that belief within your body. For example, when you write it down, do you get a feeling of dread in your stomach or your heart? A feeling of tightness? If you do, you must now ask yourself if this concept is productive or helpful to your life. If it isn't, ask yourself what would be.

Step 2

Now you have done this, you can write an affirmation that is based on the positive sides of your self-judgment. Have a thesaurus to hand so that you can find truly powerful words that will help boost your affirmations. Instead of writing, for example, "I am worthy", you could write something along the lines of, "I am a remarkable person and I am cherished:".

Once you have written your affirmation down, ask a close friend to read through it and ask them if they have any suggestions that will make your statement stronger.

Step 3

When you have your affirmation written exactly as you want it, say it aloud for a minimum of 5 minutes at a time, at least three times per day. Go for first thing in the morning, the middle of the day and last thing at night. The best times are when you are having a shave or applying makeup – look in the mirror, straight into your own eyes, and say the positive affirmation out loud.

You could also write it down several times in a notebook as this will help with the reinforcement of that belief into your subconscious. Notice that, as you write it, over the course of time, your writing style will change. This is a big clue as to how your mind is changing, as to how you are perceiving the statement and is a good chart for marking your progression

Step 4

To make sure that your affirmation is firmly anchored in your body, while you are repeating it, put your hand onto the part of your body that felt tight or uncomfortable when you write the negative statement or belief in the first step. For example, if you felt a sinking feeling in your stomach, place your hand over your stomach. Breathe deeply as you say or write your affirmation down. As your mind starts to be reprogrammed, you need to be able to move on from the original concept of that statement to the real and positive feeling of the quality you are looking for.

Step 5

Ask a good friend or a life coach to say your affirmation to you repeatedly. As they are saying, for example, "you are a remarkable person and you are cherished", you must identify that statement as a message that is "good fathering" or "good mothering". If you can't find someone that you trust to help you here, use the mirror technique and use your own reflection to reinforce that message in your mind and body.

Affirmations are incredibly powerful and can help you to change your state of mind, your mood and can help you manifest the changes that you want to bring about in your life. To make them work best, you should first identify the negative belief that is their direct opposite.

If you are finding that these suggestions are still not helping positive affirmations to work for you, it may be that you have deep-seated fears and irrationals that can only be dealt with through the help of a professionally trained therapist. It could be that you are not consciously aware of what it is, it could be buried deeply in your subconscious and must be uncovered if this is to work for you.

Mindfulness meditation is a fantastic tool that can help you to unbury unhealthy thought patterns and helps you to put them into categories, allowing you to properly identify these that are positive and those that are negative or afflicted. Mindfulness is not about changing you; it is about having the power to accept what is and then change to what is possible

Conclusion

Congratulations, you have made it to the end of this book. I hope that as you have read this book, you have found quotes and affirmations that have caused you to dig deep into yourself and find the potential buried inside. Now that you have set the foundation and begun changing your mindset, you are ready to take what you have learned and fill your life with happiness, success, and optimism.

As you move forward, remember to continue saying the affirmations that you feel speak to you the loudest. You don't want to say thirty plus affirmations a day, but choose the ones that most apply to your life and continue saying them daily. Saying affirmations every day has the power to bring great things into your life. Think about all the ways that your life has improved in the last thirty days. You are no longer the person who picked his book up a month ago. You are now more confident and ready to take on the world.

Thank you again for downloading my book, *"Positive Thinking: 30 Days Of Motivation And Affirmations: Change Your "Mindset" & Fill Your Life With Happiness, Success, & Optimism!"* I hope you enjoyed the readings in this book and wish you all the best on your continuing journey.

Help me improve this book

While I have never met you, if you made it through this book I know that you are the kind of person that is wanting to get better and is willing to take on tough feedback to get to that point. You and I are cut from the same cloth in that respect. I am always looking to get better and I wish to not just improve myself, but also this book. If you have positive feedback, please take the time to leave a review. It will help other find this book and it can help change a life in the same way that it changed yours. If you have constructive feedback, please also leave a review. It will help me better understand what you, the reader, need to make significant improvements in your life. I will take your feedback and use it to improve this book so that it can become more powerful and beneficial to all those who encounter it.

REMEMBER TO JOIN THE GROUP NOW!

If you have not joined the Mastermind Self Development group yet, now is your time! You will receive videos and articles from top authorities in self-development as well as a special group only offers on new books and training programs. There will also be a monthly member only draw that gives you a chance to win any book from your Kindle wish list!

If you sign up through this link http://www.mastermindselfdevelopment.com/specialreport you will also get a special free report on the Wheel of Life. This report will give you a visual look at your current life and then take you through a series of exercises that will help you plan what your perfect life looks like. The workbook does not end there; we then take you through a process to help you plan how to achieve that perfect life. The process is very powerful and has the potential to change your life forever. Join the group now and start to change your life!
http://www.mastermindselfdevelopment.com/specialreport

You will also love these other great titles from Mastermind Self Development!

You will want to check out these other great titles Mastermind Self Development. All available in the Kindle store or you can just click on covers below.

myBook.to/languagescombo

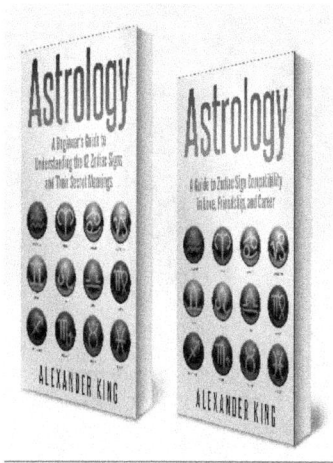

http://getbook.at/Astrology2in1

You can also find these titles by searching them in the Kindle store on Amazon.

www.ingramcontent.com/pod-product-compliance
Lightning Source LLC
Chambersburg PA
CBHW081355070526
44583CB00020B/2564